STEVE JUDD was born in the UK in July 1955. He found his first astrological tables in 1977 and then spent years learning astrological basics. He is self-taught and has written for the national press many times as well as being on the cutting edge of modern astrological developments in the last quarter of a century. In July 2005, Steve was awarded the Master of Arts Degree in Cultural Astronomy and Astrology from the Sophia Centre at Bath Spa University, the eleventh person in the world at that time to hold this qualification.

Since the late 1990s, Steve's client database has evolved exponentially. He has a loyal following, with many of his clients returning for regular updates, as well as a large presence on YouTube, with over 80,000 subscribers. He is advancing public knowledge and awareness of astrology like no other before him in modern times.

In more than forty years of study and practise as an astrologer, Steve has developed unique ways of interpreting the horoscope. He covers all pertinent areas involving health patterns, children, residence, family, finances, community, career, philosophy and relationships, as well as working extensively with astrolocation. Steve's ability to define and explain past situations from an impersonal and objective perspective gives him the potential to expand on current situations and then explore and project into possible options for the future.

For more information, visit these websites: www.stevejudd.co, and www.astrobabbleproductions.com.

D1646101

THE BEDROOM
ASTROLOGER

A between-the-sheets users guide to the
sexual preferences of each sign of the Zodiac

STEVE JUDD

SilverWood

Published in 2023 by SilverWood Books

SilverWood Books Ltd
14 Small Street, Bristol, BS1 1DE, United Kingdom
www.silverwoodbooks.co.uk

ISBN 978-1-80042-051-9 (paperback)

British Library Cataloguing in Publication Data
A CIP catalogue record for this book is
available from the British Library

Page design and typesetting by SilverWood Books

Contents

Introduction

How to use this book

This book is not only about sex in its various different manifestations, it is also about astrology at a number of different levels and how sex and astrology blend and interact. The reader will need to know an absolute basic minimum about astrology, although a copy of your horoscope is always an advantage. This minimum knowledge breaks down into four words: Planets, Signs, Houses and Aspects and the following is a one paragraph long user guide to these words.

Planets are bodies of rock or gas in space orbiting around the Sun with each planet relating to a particular type of energy. For example, one planet may symbolically represent all forms of communication whilst another shows how we use our physical energy. Each planet is in a sign of the zodiac at the time of birth and the zodiac sign influence shows the way that the planet manifests its energy. If the planet of communication is in a water sign then a basic meaning of this would be that communication is primarily influenced by the emotions whereas in an air sign communication would be more influenced by the intellect. As the signs of the zodiac show the way that planetary energies manifest in and through the individual, so the houses of the zodiac show the ways that the planetary energies manifest themselves in the eyes of others in the outside world. Planets in signs are how you behave; planets in houses are how you are seen to behave. Aspects are the geometric angles existing between planets with some angles creating specific patterns of harmonics and other angles doing the opposite, creating patterns of dynamics (astrologers used to say good and bad but now say harmonic and dynamic). To summarise:

Planets represent individual energies
Zodiac signs show how we use and demonstrate that energy
Zodiac houses show how that energy is used in the eyes of the outside world
Aspects show how we help and hinder ourselves

A basic knowledge of your horoscope will greatly benefit your understanding and interaction with this book. If you only know your horoscope Sun sign (Aries, Virgo etc.) you may find yourself disadvantaged as in many cases the Sun may be the only point in your sign whilst there may be four or five planets in the next door sign, creating a very different influence. This is the origin of the perennial complaint, "But I'm nothing like what the books say I am…"

Ideally you will have an understanding of the basic pattern of your chart, knowing the sign positions of the Sun, Venus and Mars, as well as (hopefully) Uranus, Neptune and Pluto and the angles and aspects between these planets.

This book is aimed at three different levels of astrological student. Initially it is aimed at the novice, the beginner and the idle curiosity seeker who wants to dip into something light that will bring humour into their or their partner's life. This is where the first section of the book based on a generalised Sun sign description can be most useful. It is great for reading out loud at drunken parties etc…it's a laugh folks and purely meant as that. Secondly the sections on Venus and Mars are aimed at the more knowledgeable student who will recognise patterns amongst those they know and have charts for and learn from that observation and thirdly, this book is aimed at those researchers who are trying to redefine the meanings of the outer planets and their aspects from a more twenty-first century perspective.

This book is composed of three sections: The first section relates to the twelve signs of the zodiac and their typical energies. The signs are grouped in pairs of opposites, as will be seen in the index. 'Opposites attract' is an old adage that works well here. Opposites also reflect, showing each sign what it is missing. For example, have you ever really met a grounded Pisces? Or a Virgo with imagination? Or a detached Leo? Or a passionate Aquarius? Each chapter compares one sign of the zodiac to its opposite in terms of how these people express their needs, wants and desires in the sensual and sexual arena. It shows what turns these people on, what stimuli works for them, how they act and react, what they expect and hope for and how they play the subtle and not so subtle games of love and lust. Each chapter incorporates the following sub sections:

Bedroom etiquette
How to enjoy food
Location, location
How to pamper them
Favourite fantasies
What they really, really want
What to watch out for
How to wind them up

The second section describes the influences and effects of Venus and Mars in the signs and houses of the zodiac as well as translating the influences they have upon each other by aspect. It is a somewhat light-hearted look at how Venus and Mars relate to the male/female and projective/receptive sides of our natures and shows the ways in which we like to be treated and the ways we take action both in and out of the bedroom.

The third section shows the influences made by Uranus, Neptune and Pluto in our charts. These outer planets show the more hidden, unconscious and subconscious side of our nature and the ways in which they aspect Venus and Mars can be specifically related to sensual and sexual attitudes, patterns, tastes, complexes and neuroses. By looking at the sign and house of the zodiac that Venus and Mars were in at the time of your birth and considering the aspects made by them to the outer planets it is possible to understand the basic mechanics of what gives every one of us our potential uniqueness in the bedroom.

This book does not cover all of the astrological factors involved in the making of a horoscope. There is no reference here to Mercury (communication), Jupiter (growth), or Saturn (structure). There is also no reference to the Ascendant or the Midheaven, the Moon or the Sun except in the first part of the book which covers the generalised sun sign positions. The Sun and the Moon provide the greater framework to which the area of sensuality and sexuality is but a portion. To discuss the full meanings of the Sun/Moon interactions at a more than sensual/sexual level goes beyond the scope of this book. It would take up too much space, folks! However, this book does cover the meaning of the twelve houses of the zodiac, loosely relating to the twelve signs but in a more physically manifest and demonstrable way.

1

The Houses of the Zodiac

A brief explanation

The first house relating to Aries is the house of the individuality and the self. Planets in the first house bring a sense of uniqueness and identity into the make-up and create an energy field conducive to dynamic, projective and assertive action, although there can also be the tendency to act before one thinks and to jump in head first. It is the space in the horoscope for self-determination; it is where one can be at your most confrontational but also most effective through the process of direct action.

Actions speak louder than words for these pushy and impulsive people, their philosophy is "Don't tell me what you are going to do, tell me when you have done it" and at the end of the day they value material and physical developments and actions more than ideas or words. Head bangers on the side they are the proactive ones in the bedroom, preferring to take the initiative as opposed to waiting for someone else to do it.

Passionate and physical, it is sometimes as though the bedroom is a war zone with conquests to be made. Only when they have demonstrated their power enough do they let their childlike soul relax and only when they realise that they are in no danger from their partner do they finally stop trying so hard to impress. The raunchiest and most projective sexual house of the zodiac, planets here make you try harder to meet your (sometimes unrealistic) expectations of both yourself and others.

The second house relating to Taurus is the house of value and worth. It is about possessions in terms of finances, goods, chattels, materials and it is about the way that you value these things and the people who come with them. What has value and worth? People with lots of planets in the second house tend to find that as they get older so material security fades in importance. If value and worth used to be measured in terms of financial security and stability, possessions and material welfare, then as one ages so your values tend to move more towards the non-material, becoming steadily more a matter of spiritual, ethical and moral value and worth both internally and externally.

The more evolved types know the value of integrity and dignity and they realise as they mature that you can't take it with you and it is not how much you have got as what you do with it that counts in the long run. In the bed chamber this idea of value and worth extends into their partner, where they often value and rate their own performance through the eyes of the significant other. When young, these people can be quite possessive and jealous of their partners and only when they age do they realise that they cannot actually own anyone else but they can own the memories of sharing with that person, something that ultimately brings more pleasure and warmth than simple possession.

The third house relates to Gemini and is known as the house of communications and movement, especially in terms of localised movement, whether that is done with the brain, mouth or body. It governs all areas of localised travel and neighbourly interactions and influences not only the amount of wordage but also the quality of what comes out of the mouth. The third house also has a lot to do with interactions at the day by day level, especially with siblings or with those who fulfil that role, people with whom one is in fairly regular constant daily contact. People with a lot of planets in the third house tend to collect things, words and people. They always have an extensive address book and an overflowing diary and always seem hideously overburdened and over detailed. They would do well to stop occasionally for ten seconds and take deep breaths. They like lots of distractions, toys and knick-knacks in the bedroom, the more the merrier. Anything to spread their attention whilst you concentrate on your lover will enhance your sexual performance, although if they get too sidelined by curiosity you may find that you get bored with superficiality and go elsewhere. Third house individuals talk a good talk but the wise ones know when to just shut up and let their hands and bodies do their talking for them, knowing that the tongue isn't only for talking with.

The fourth house relates to Cancer, the sign of the home and is directly related to issues of not only home and family but also things concerning security, safety and your ability to provide comfort and warmth to both yourself and those that depend on you. Here is where the home fires burn strongest, where the warmest fireside and bed lie and where you can always be sure of a restful and relaxing stay. The fourth house also relates to one or both of the parents in terms of the way that you were nurtured (or not) as a child and the way that you project that nurturing capacity into the outside world as you mature. It gives a root and base to the chart that provides secure foundations, whether they are bricks and mortar or whether they are emotional and/or psychological.

The fourth house is where you can close the door and no one can come in without your permission and this degree of privacy extends into the personal life as well, as what goes on in the bedroom stays in the bedroom. Strangely enough, fourth house individuals are the most extreme in the bed chamber. They either shut up shop and quickly develop platonic relationships primarily based just on hugs and cuddles, or else they go to the other end of the spectrum in that they can be the kinkiest and rudest lovers imaginable. Unless you are privileged enough to share their bedroom, you are never going to really know what makes these sensitive souls tick.

The fifth house relating to Leo is traditionally known as the house of creativity and the most common example of creativity is through procreativity, hence children. Their children are likely to be the apple of their eye, in many ways the single biggest and most important thing in life. If childless, then the creative projects and artistic impressions will become almost like the baby, something that they imbue themselves with through creative self-development. The fifth house is also known as the area of romance, pleasure and fun, although long term relationships are governed by another house.

The fifth house is where you can be playful, where you play for the fun of playing as opposed to competition. It is where you can bring humour and bounce into your life and the lives of those around you. This childlike (childlike, not childish) attitude extends into the area of sense and sexuality. These playful souls love being stroked, caressed, tickled and generally touched in a loving way and they are quite happy to return the favour. Strangely enough, they are not that concerned about the full degree of intimacy, sometimes just content to roll around and writhe in anticipation, they just cannot take sex seriously. It has to have a degree of humour about it or it's not worth doing.

The sixth house, relating to Virgo is known as the house of health. Sub headings are the house of duty, service and responsibility for those less fortunate than yourself, as well as the area concerning not only health but also hygiene and diet. If you have a lot of planets in this house it indicates the need to be of service, for your work to benefit others as much as yourself. Just remember that you are a servant not a slave and that you do things for others because you want to, not because others want you to. Otherwise you start to feel obliged and taken for granted and then it's seriously time to walk away before you become the victim of your own martyrdom.

These people are the busy bees of the zodiac, always doing something. They don't feel comfortable unless they have a piece of paper handy to put all their lists down on, they do lists big time, it helps them stay in order. They like the bed sheets to be ironed and wrinkle free, at least at the start of the evening and the idea of biscuit crumbs in the bed is the worst thing imaginable, a real turn off. Not that impressed by perfumes or superficial gloss, these secret earthy fantasists get right down to the basic functionality of sex almost from the word go, bringing a healthy, holistic and integrated approach to sex, with built in ethics and morals.

The Libran orientated seventh house of one-to-one relationships does just what it says on the label and that is dealing with things and people at the one-to-one level, whether through friend, partner, family, social, professional or other. If you have got lots of planets here, you may find yourself at times almost dependent on others for stimulation to the point of neediness. Alternatively, and probably at the same time, you will find that people gravitate towards you at the one-to-one level almost as if you are their counsellor or therapist. The downside of this is dependency; the upside is synergy, where two people working together are better than working apart. Or two and two equals five, if that is any clearer.

This is the best place in the heavens as far as being with 'other' is concerned, although sometimes there is a clear need for that level of diplomacy and subtlety to stop dead at the door of the bedroom because blandness doesn't work so well with passion. This is the best position in the heavens for genuinely wanting to please the partner without thought of reward or return, because pleasing your partner equates to pleasing yourself. These are the bedroom sophisticates, the gentle and refined. Coarse and gross people need not apply.

The eighth house, relating to the sign of Scorpio has the craziest reputation of all the houses. According to the old text books it is the house of sex, death and transformation but from a more modernistic perspective it's the area of your chart that deals with external resources and systems of power. It can represent partner's money and joint resources, bank loans, mortgages or tax rebates, inheritances or other forms of external funding, i.e. sponsorship or investment. It also has to do with the more psychological side of life that involves research and digging deep and because of this is associated with the darker side of life. The real eighth house person knows that darkness is only the absence of light and that they can work with both and it is only really shades of grey that cause problems. They are psychologists in the bedroom as well, not content unless they have investigated every nook and cranny of your body, mind and soul. If you let them in, you will find that they give it back threefold and unconditionally. They will trust totally and forever if they get the same back and the enlightened ones learn to forgive, if not forget. They will take you to the pits and the heights and you will have fun and possibly also pain on both journeys. Just don't expect these people to be middle of the road.

The Sagittarian orientated ninth house is known as the house that deals with religion, belief systems, higher education and large-scale or long-term foreign travel. All of these things deal with the idea of expanding the mind, reaching out for further knowledge in terms of direct experience as opposed to learning by rote or from teachers or text books. With the travel, it is not so much arriving at the destination or what you do when you are there, it's the journey and it is the same with any higher educational course.

This is the area of your chart where you find your own relationship with the divine however you conceive it as being and how you live life according to your own beliefs and laws, hopefully not too dissimilar to the norm. The ninth house is where you find your own personal truth systems and it is how you walk your talk. Admittedly, it is a bit disconcerting when you stop halfway through sex to comment on a philosophical viewpoint and you definitely need a partner who is your intellectual equal and can appreciate the humorous and the ridiculous side of sex. Nevertheless, this is the best position in the zodiac for letting your higher mind guide the more physical patterns; these are the people who investigate Tanta, meditation, yoga and other forms of spiritual and sexual development on their quest for understanding a higher meaning in life.

The tenth house, equivalent to the sign of Capricorn is normally known as the house of career but this is a loose term. Certainly this is the area of work, career, ambition and goals, it is the way that you interact at the professional level in the workplace but it is also closely related to concepts such as public image, profile, visibility and the way that you project yourself into and onto the outside world. The tenth house also governs the ways that you interact with all systems of authority in your outside world life, ranging from God and the different forms of your employer on the one hand to the school teacher and the parent on the other. It is the outside world and its effects on you as much as your role in that external pattern and the wise ones of this group quickly orchestrate their outside world into a system that works for them.

This pattern of assuming authority and responsibility for their outside world life also extends into the bedroom, at least until clear boundaries are set and adhered to. These are the people who constantly push buttons and constraints in order to establish clear guidelines of behaviour. It is only when these boundaries are mutually recognized that these secretly timid souls can really relax and enjoy intimacy, safe and secure in each other's arms.

The Aquarian influenced eleventh house is known universally as the house of community. Here is where you find your true tribe and family, regardless of blood links. Community can be personal, as in the close friendships that you build over the years and come to love and trust simply because of commonality. Community can also be in the local arena in terms of clubs, societies and the loose fraternities you associate with. Of course, there is the idea of the global community and your awareness of your role in it.

People with an abundance of eleventh house energy generally tend to focus themselves into helping others as much as if not more than themselves, knowing that being of use to the larger group brings more personal reward than working solely for yourself. It is no good trying to grab these people for your personal and private lover. Of course they will stay honest and true but they need social contact with others to constantly assess what it is about you compared to others that turns them on. If they find themselves too isolated from community, they tend to turn inwards and become nuns or monks. Of all the positions in the zodiac, this is the strongest for celibacy as a form of purity. At the other end of the spectrum, the lower evolved types will have many ongoing attachments at various levels of intimacy, often at the same time but these people generally tend to lose friends fast.

The twelfth house, with its affiliation with Pisces is generally known as the house of the unconscious, the dream, the vision and the intuitive capacity. It is where the conscious mind doesn't work and you have to learn to trust the gut instinct, the intuition and the sixth and seventh senses as well as the second and third thoughts. It is where there is an occasional need for solitude, for sitting by where the sea and the sand join, walking alone in the woods or standing on top of a hill and just being with the world and the universe.

Obviously, notions of individual identity are hard to sustain here and these souls can be so gullible that they fall for every sob story in their desire to help the world, so they need time alone every day in order to gather themselves together and maintain a working relationship with the outside world. In the bedroom, these are the real surrender junkies, being at their best with their partner in the dark under the quilt, or deep in the cave at some level. They are the very best at just going with the flow, as well as flowing with the go and they all secretly want nothing more than to live a Jane Austen lifestyle. When these romantic dreamers come down to earth and actually create their visions, they are the artists of the zodiac.

2

Aries–Libra

'I am you and you are me and we are all together...'

Bedroom etiquette

When it comes to bedroom etiquette no other sign combination demonstrates the theory of opposites better than Aries and Libra. So polarised yet so similar in their ultimate desire, to be loved. The essence of Aries is that of the perennial infant, crying "Me! Me! Me!" all the time. Their reputation for selfishness and egocentric behaviour is well known and, in some cases, even valid. It is not that they are really selfish; it's just that their known universe extends to about four millimetres beyond their nose and the next fifteen minutes. The more enlightened ones, the ones who have made an effort to grow up (and I am not talking about physical age here) have made the realisation that the quality of their bedroom experience can actually be magnified and expanded if they spare some of their precious time to consider the needs and enjoyment of their partners.

The essence of Libra is the total opposite. They can't possibly put their wants and needs before anyone else's because that is just not fair. They work on the principle that life is meaningless unless they are in a relationship to the point that some of these delicate people suffer greatly for their partners to the point of subservience. There are the 'soggy' Librans, who simply cannot make a decision without consulting everyone else, who in the long run become so imbalanced by other people's pull on them that they become extremists themselves and then there are the balanced Librans, the ones who make sure that they get their fair share and who know how to establish and maintain their boundaries whilst reassuring others at the same time about theirs.

The typical Aries bed partner typifies all that one might expect of these Mars ruled warriors, with a philosophy of "Right! Let's get our clothes off, jump into bed and get on with it, yes?" on the grounds that actions speak louder than words. They cannot be dallying around with lots of fripperies, teasing and guessing games, they haven't got time for that. When love and lust combine these people aren't going to waste time analysing and contemplating when they could be in the throes of passion because the moment might slip away if they are not quick enough. On the other hand, Libra enjoys all the dressing up and undressing, the subtle little nuances, the gentle and subtle art of mutual seduction. Most Librans dislike the cut and thrust attitude to the point of turnoff and rejection. They like taking their time and slowly discovering each other. The typical Aries will tumble into bed at a moment's notice, throwing their clothes in a trail to the bedroom, whilst the Libra person will plan the evening meal, enjoy a good wine and languidly suggest they retire to a place where they can become more comfortable (and hang up their clothes).

Location, location

When it comes to location, again these signs reflect the opposite of each other. To a person with a large amount of Aries energy in their horoscope it doesn't really matter at all about location, a magnificent bedroom with all the trimmings is essentially just as good as a kitchen floor, the sofa, in the barn or in the woods. Aries do have a preference for outdoor activity more than any other sign of the zodiac although given the choice anywhere with a mattress or other form of padding will do. It is the urgency and the immediacy of the moment that Aries crave. The location is secondary to the sensation.

To Librans, location is everything. Not for them an alleyway or the back seat of a car. They want the sophistication and elegance of the four-poster bed, satin sheets, low lighting and dreamy background music, lots of drapes and cushions and room service to boot. They need to feel comfortable and at ease with their situation and if they don't get at least half of what they want then they are going to shut up shop.

How to enjoy food

When it comes to matters of taste then the Aries and Libra personalities are about as different as you get. There seems to be truth in the adage that Aries will eat anything if it is served with chillies. Certainly they like hot food with ginger, chilli, hot curries, cayenne peppers and garlic predominating. They also go for bright colours like red, yellow and orange. Parsnip and cabbage soup would seriously depress these fire eaters. The famous Arian impatience streak extends to the kitchen and if they could get away with it they would live on fast food. A word to the wise. Don't get between a hungry Aries and their food. Strangely enough, Aries are not that inventive with food in the bedroom. Show them a courgette or a peach and their first impulse is to eat it. They like their sex raw and to the point, no culinary skills are needed.

Librans have style. They may not have class but they have got style. Librans like their curry mild. Their palate is subtle, ranging from artichoke hearts to pate de foie gras and truffles, cognac and blue mountain coffee. When that selection is not available they will happily settle for what is as long as it is well garnished and presented. The environment and the setting for the meal are important. The one thing to remember about Librans is that they don't like to eat alone because that's when the snacks, biscuits and the sandwiches come out. Their culinary skills match their bedroom ones. In the bedroom they have a fondness for mushy fruit of all types, the juicier the better. They like to feel squishy in moments of intimacy and what better than a ripe mango or banana to help this process along?

How to pamper them

Once again Aries is pretty unidirectional here. If it is to do with the physical body, then that's fine. Concentrate on making them feel good – literally! Give them a brisk rub down with a loofah. If you can give good massage then that is a long way down the road to them loving you more in one fell swoop. It will have to be Rolfing, deep tissue or Swedish massage though as there is nothing wishy-washy about these brave souls, they like it pro-active. They have to learn by gradual experience about the more subtle and sensual side of massage. You have to let them win sometimes so let them have it their way, let them get on top every so often, play up to their inner child occasionally.

If you are in the mood to buy them anything, it doesn't matter what you give them as long as it is new. They don't have a lot of patience for things that are older than them and it is possible that this could include you! It is wise to flatter them occasionally because after all everyone needs to be told that they are liked and that they are cool and to Aries being at the forefront of your mind really makes them feel good.

Being told that they are liked and wanted is also at the very top of Libra's list. They more than any other sign can actually time their orgasms to coincide with their partners. If that isn't a perfect example of the Libran desire for sharing and equality, then I don't know what is. They also go for massage in a big way but of a much more gentle, receptive and aesthetic type. Their reasoning is that this normally lasts a lot longer and is thus more pleasurable. A word to the wise in that some Librans can get so engrossed in the physical sensation of being massaged that they can easily fall asleep, bringing an early end to any other plans that they or their partners may have had.

Go out of your way occasionally to put their wants and desires first. Nibble their ears or blow (gently!) in them. Compliment them on their elegance and their sophistication in the public eye as well as in the bedroom. Make them feel wanted and loved and you will find that they go along with ninety-five per cent of what you suggest. Just don't ever, ever put them on the spot and insist that they make a decision for the both of you right there and then. For some strange reason, they all seem to like having their toes and feet rubbed.

Favourite fantasies

Aries of both genders enjoy the hunt and often the bedroom is the arena or stage for the event. Both men and women have conquest as a buzz word in their fantasies. The men dream of being the Viking 'berserker' and the women of being the Amazon. If there is no competition in their love life, no test of challenge, endurance or power, if there is no fun then they can go off people very fast. They like constant stimulation and providing they get it they will always give a lot more in return. The desire for thrills and excitement and the fun of the chase makes these hardy people the best outdoor lovers (an isolated woodland setting is recommended), although given the choice they will always take a deep pile rug in front of a blazing fire armed with nothing but red wine, a bowl of cherries and fresh strawberries. Self-centred, yes. Selfish, no.

Librans love to be flattered, complimented and purred over, nibbled, tickled and gently lulled into that sense of easy-goingness where life just seems so amenable. Although some of them are as tough as old boots they all like to be pampered and worshipped. They dream of candlelit bedrooms with soft music, a large four-poster bed with hanging drapes, gentle music and a partner who kisses them constantly and murmurs sweet nothing into their ears whilst they slowly remove each other's clothes. Mr and Miss Sensuality to everyone else except fellow Librans they will happily go along with whatever is happening as long as there is a degree of sharing and balance. Bedroom aids for the typical Libra include cocoa butter, lots of massage oil and loads of chocolate. No-one else is as good as them at looking demure and helpless whilst getting you to do what they wanted all along without you even realising it until afterwards.

What they really, really want

Here the opposites have gone full circle and met each other on the other side in that they both have an insatiable desire to be loved and wanted. Aries has an almost childlike attitude towards self-gratification whilst Libra craves that emotional bonding that true sharing brings.

You can smooth your way into the Aries inner sanctum in almost any circumstances by complimenting them on their appearance and their physique. They thrive on being adored and as long as they are the centre of your passion and affection then you have them hooked. Once that has happened, they discover a talent for excitement and variation that gets stronger as they get older so do nice things to remind them that you love them and they will always follow you home.

Libra likes to imagine itself as being elegant at all times and compliments to this effect are always popular. They are the world champions at sensuality, so delicate, sensitive and gentle but assertive behaviour always works. They are willing and even eager to let other people make the decisions as well as most of the leading moves as long as it's something that they want to do. They need to be stroked in such a way that makes them purr. Give them the best to remind them how much you value them.

What to watch out for

Aries can easily allow flattery to develop into narcissism. Sure, they like to be admired and reminded how special they are to you but after a time they start to believe it all a little too much and the eternal child comes through saying "I want – and if I don't get I will scream till I die!" At times they can be self-centred to the point of blind egotism, so it is necessary to bring them down to earth occasionally by doing what you want, regardless of their tears. Words like irresponsibility, childishness, selfishness and egotism describe the Aries monster that lurks within. Slow them down in the bedroom, show them how things can sometimes be a lot better when they take their time and are not so impulsive and impatient. Once the ego goes beyond the confines of the bedroom then things can get out of hand and suddenly you are stuck with an eight-year-old in an adult body.

Libra makes a life career of being indecisive. "I don't know." "What do you think?" "Where shall we go?" "What shall I wear?" "It's up to you. You decide." These are all common catchphrases for them. They will do (almost) anything to be loved and they often need to be persuaded to take decisions for themselves. Remind them about keywords such as equality and sharing and don't criticise them when they are wrong. These people smoulder in the bedroom like a fire that is red hot inside but covered in a deceptive layer of grey ash, they start to glow when blown on. When they are hot they stay hot for a long, long time. Encourage them to take the initiative sometimes or run the risk of them becoming laid back to the point of falling asleep.

How to wind them up

The easiest way to antagonise an Aries is to totally ignore them, to forget to introduce them to your friends and to make them feel as though they don't matter and that they are insignificant. You could try being kind to their enemies but that's tantamount to treason and probably won't ever be forgiven. You can also try informing them of their childish and even their infantile ways but all they will do is stick their noses in the air and ignore you.

Whereas with Libra, apart from making them decide everything the key thing to do is to act gross when out with them in public. Wipe your nose on your sleeve when with them. Take them to heavy metal or punk gigs. They pride themselves on their aestheticism and sensitivity so the coarser you act the more it gets their goat. They are generally all lousy at making on the spot decisions, preferring to sit on the fence and occupy the moral middle ground. Of course, if you really want to upset them take them to the cheapest of restaurants.

3

Taurus–Scorpio

'Be careful what you wish for, lest it come true...'

Bedroom etiquette

It is a Mexican stand-off sort of thing, with each of you daring the other to go just that little bit further. Always asking yourselves (and each other!) about what has worth, does it turn you on, whether you are valued enough, does it feel good or where is the next sensation coming from. Whilst neither of you have a monopoly on sensuality, the pair of you react more physically than any other sign of the zodiac. It's true that you really do live in your body and most intimate relationships develop into a 'push me pull you' sort of thing where physical magnetism or repulsion becomes as strong as, if not stronger than, the intuition.

Taurus particularly has an affinity with the stomach. There is no point whatsoever dragging a Taurean to bed if they are physically hungry. You just won't perform, your 'love engine' is located firmly in the stomach and you can't run on empty. Even half full is a bit sluggish, as concentration on matters in hand can easily lose focus if the belly is rumbling. A healthy compromise is to integrate foodstuffs into the bedroom on the grounds that you can always eat what you don't have any other use for but remember that the sensation's the thing and some of the best sexual organs are located very close indeed to the taste buds. Most Taureans will have an emergency energy bar tucked away in the bedside drawer for a snack at three in the morning and are more inclined to the tasteful (literally!) types of bedroom aids and toys.

Scorpio's area exists below the stomach. The really powerful Scorpios know that I'm not talking about the genitals but the area about three inches above and one inch behind. Like Taurus the physical senses rule and in the bedroom the senses start in the midriff and head south. The emphasis on feeling is so strong that many Scorpios genuinely do prefer the dark or the half-light in the bedroom or at least pulling the blankets over your head. This sign of extremes can live up to its reputation in the bedroom ranging from the scared and inhibited to the truly sensual and passionate. Power issues are never far away with some Scorpios becoming overly concerned about control and dominance. The wise Scorpios know that power flows through them, that they can express it but not own and control it. This brings a whole new meaning to the word powerfull (sic).

With both Taurus and Scorpio, the sensation is the thing. The whole body is an erogenous zone to be stroked, pampered, adored, tickled, fondled and loved and the more 'icky' and 'gooey' it gets the better.

Location, location

With both of these signs the body is the thing so the doing of the deed can sometimes take more precedence than the location. Both Taurus and Scorpio like it sensual so angles and sharp corners are out of the question. 'Snug' is a word that describes the desired ambience, although the actual physical situations vary greatly as might be expected by these two opposite signs.

Taurus, with its capacity for being earthy is not known for its fussiness about location. Any barn, field, forest glade, haystack, tent or such like will do. They do like to be in touch with the earth as it makes them feel more secure in a weird type of way. Getting muddy or dirty during the process can be seen as a bonus, there is a kind of bonding with the planet during sex that links them with what they conceive of as being 'Mother Earth' and creates a more ethnic vibe.

It is really important for these grounded and materialistic people to feel that they are in touch and on planet during love making although this can be compensated for by lots of cuddles and hugs. A warm and luxurious mud spa would be the ideal situation for these comfort lovers as long as food was within easy reach but Taurus is very much a fan of rutting season (May – April) so anywhere will do as long as there is a degree of comfort. Can you feel the love?

Scorpio likes it personal and intimate and can be exceptionally choosy about location. Their reputation for secrecy is somewhat overstated but certainly there is a desire for privacy. Somewhere cloistered and intimate is preferable ideally with a dimmer switch so that lighting levels can be adjusted at will. Privacy is important; to Scorpio the idea of being surprised or caught in the act is repugnant, therefore a door lock is essential. The old story about Scorpio doing it in the dark is rooted in truth, they prefer the dark because without sight the other senses are heightened and Scorpio is nothing if not sensual. Buried deep under the duvet or for that matter in a car or any enclosed space or somewhere else that suggests seclusion is where they are at their most intimate.

How they enjoy food

There is an inverse ratio pattern that clearly demonstrates whether a Taurean is enjoying food and that's clearly demonstrated by how much noise they make when they are eating. More likely than any other sign of the zodiac to groan and moan with pleasure, the filling of the mouth with the added bonus of taste is heaven sent to these passionate foodophiles. A key thing is the amount. Quality is one thing but quantity is quite another and potatoes in any form are always a sure bet. If you can't get potatoes, then some type of stodge, i.e. rice, pasta, bread etc. A bird in the hand is worth two in the bush works in this case, you can always tempt a Taurus with food. Wait until they are peckish and then lead them upstairs with a punnet of cherries or strawberries, some ice-cream and honey and they will follow you anywhere! Think of the toddler running around with food in their hands and a messy mouth, who'll eat anything they find.

How do Scorpios enjoy food? Secretly! They are the 3am fridge raider and like their Cancerian cousins they squirrel titbits of food away for later perusal and taste. Dark chocolate, liquorice, coffee (dark) all work, they like to dissect their meals and can be very selective. They eat a lot of eliminative foods such as chilli, garlic and ginger, as well as dried fruits on the grounds that they like to be regular. No one can accuse them of being anal. Their reputation for cleansing, purifying and getting rid of waste is well deserved. You can always spot a Scorpio in a bad mood at the dinner table because they are the ones holding the knife just a little bit too tightly whilst staring at their fish and mushroom pate as if they are daring it to move.

How to pamper them

We return again to the land of sensuality where sensations are the real deal, where the touch, taste, feel, sight and sound of things really do turn these physically passionate and erotically charged people on, it's a body thing. Both Taurus and Scorpio view their body as their temple so anything that complements their physical well-being will be warmly appreciated.

Taureans philosophies are based on simplicity. Pleasure and practicality rule, if it feels good and it doesn't cost the earth then why not especially if you enjoy it. They love all types of massage although the deeper and more muscular forms have the strongest effects. Taureans love being oiled with exotic substances, the more the merrier although sensual oils like patchouli or musk work best. They are a cross between Adonis (adore me! adore me!) and Bacchus (eat, drink and be merry!).

Taureans love being fed large and exotic dishes to their hearts content. They like going places where the seats are large and plush. Taurus like to feel secure at all levels so occasionally shower them in dollar bills or ten-pound notes and don't worry, they will find every one of them in the morning. If you want to buy them anything, a general rule of thumb is the bigger the better as subtleties are wasted on most Taureans. They like their comfort so a pleasant and comfortable location is as important as the actual event. Food, health spas, treats, money or anything that makes them feel good with the emphasis on the feeling. Avoid anything plastic as they like to have a modicum of taste and some things are just too trashy.

In a kind of weird way Scorpios enjoy making it hard for others to pamper them. The end result isn't as important as the effort involved. They like to be mildly scared so take them for long night-time walks at the new Moon. Scorpio cultivates a sense of mystique where the game they play is 'I dare you to suss me out'. Give them a sense or feeling of power in the bedroom so that they can play at taking and surrendering control. They all like private dinners in secluded restaurants, they do suave and sophisticated very well but can switch at a moment's notice to gauche and swarthy.

If you really trust them let them tickle you with the tip of their sting then they will never leave you. When it comes to gifts the wrapping and the intent with which it is given is more important than the content. Scorpios like black and purple with occasional scarlet flashes, velvet and satin often work as presents. Alternatively, they do Velcro everything. They don't do flamboyance and chic because they do style, just don't stand them up in public and always tell the truth, because they know if you are lying.

Favourite fantasies

Taurean fantasies generally revolve around pampering their bodies and stimulating their senses. The more adventurous of them want to coat their partners' bodies in honey and take their time licking it off. Remember the scene from the rock-opera *Tommy* of Ann-Margaret wallowing luxuriously in a bath of baked beans? I bet that was written by a Taurus. Food as well as soft gooey warm mud-like stuff in the same breath. Paradise. They really like 'doing it' al fresco accompanied by much beating of the chest and grunting. Alternatively, creature comforts are the easiest way into these physical and sensual people's hearts and anything involving food, lotions, oils, massage and to an extent size are guaranteed to open their boundaries as long as there is substance and not just lip service. (?!)

Scorpio and fantasy? Such a thing needs to be handled with wrought iron gloves and ceramic smoked glass masks. Fear is temptation, the dark stimulates and terrifies at the same time. To dominate or be dominated, to be powerful or powerless, to tantalise and tease and to keep yourself and others in suspense. To Scorpio a form of orgasm is the greatest feeling in the world and ideally they would be constantly in this state of bliss. They all live in a world where they are constantly aware of the taboos of sexual etiquette but to them half the fun is breaking those taboos. They can't help it; they have a button that gets pushed every time they hear the words "You wouldn't dare."

Thing is, they extol their price in the long run and invariably the perpetrator of the dare ends up coming off worse so weigh the karma involved before pushing Scorpio's buttons too much.

What they really, really want

Both signs complement each other here as sensation is the thing and the body the tool through which these sensations are felt. Physical pleasure is the highest of feelings, whether that is through cuddles, food, sex or other forms of feel good factors. Taurus and Scorpio are both of the opinion that the body is a temple and should be worshipped at every given opportunity.

Taureans particularly are hot on the physical sensations in that they all secretly want to be adored, loved, nurtured, pampered, fed and cuddled in random order and as often as possible! Not only do they wish for these things, they also crave to do the same things for others. Taurus is generally seen as the best there is in the kitchen, there is a compassionate and nurturing side to their nature which makes them want to feed the world. It all comes down to issues of value and Taurus wants to be wanted and valued or needed even. It makes them feel useful and part of what is going on around them. Providing their own personal needs are met they are the world's best at providing and being there for others.

What Scorpio really wants is to be safe. The outer image of needing to be in control or to be controlled is just that, an outer image. They just want to be held, comforted, cuddled and treated as though they are the most important person on the planet. They like to feel desired and the kinkier of the breed will go to any lengths to fulfil that ambition. All Scorpios ideally crave a relationship where they can safely let out their anger and passion without having to justify or explain themselves, without having to have reasons for their feelings or actions, to be unreasonable! It is only when they don't feel safe enough to naturally express themselves that things can get a little warped or twisted so give them a place in your heart, your bedroom or/ and your life and they will be there forever.

What to watch out for

The old adage about Taureans being possessive is based on truth. They can become so insecure about themselves that they will cling to anything or anyone whom they think will nurture or care for them. To Taurus, property, possessions and money represent external manifestations of an internal need to be safe and in the absence of a warm and secure fostering and nurturing environment they can and often do attach themselves to the more materialistic side of life. Consequently, bank balance can sometimes be ahead of love in the desire for security and often these solid and grounded people turn to food, especially comfort eating as an antidote to the unpredictability of love and relationships, which in turn leads to an ever-expanding waistline. The image of the round and jolly Taurean is only a metaphor for the expansiveness of western society. It is the thin Taureans to watch out for as they are sharper and more in touch with their feelings and they know the real values of the world.

The warning about the Scorpion's sting is just hype in most cases. There are generally three types of Scorpios. There is the dove Scorpio who will kill you with kindness whilst making it perfectly clear that they are suffering but it really doesn't matter. There is the Scorpion Scorpio who will get even come what may and no matter how long it takes and these are the ones you really don't want to upset. Then there is the eagle Scorpio who constantly strives and struggles to elevate their consciousness without offending anyone else. All three of these categories go through their own private hell at various times in their lives and many of them learn the true secret of power, that it is not theirs to control but only to act as a conduit for, to channel energy and power constructively. It is basically down to the difference between your needs, wants and desires with the lower evolved not getting beyond the desire stage.

How to wind them up

To alienate a Taurus, you have to get them where it hurts, in their physical values. Borrow money from them and 'forget' to return it, eat all of their food. Use their valued possessions flippantly. Accuse them of being jealous or possessive and even if not true it will still hit home somewhere. Keep telling them to hurry up and that they are too slow. Taurus likes to establish a tempo, a pace which they can then maintain. The worst insult is to label them as being boring.

To wind up a Scorpio can be seen as being either brave or foolish. A good way to upset them is to tell them that they are paranoid and that everyone really is talking about them behind their back. You could suggest that they are secretive although the savvy ones will reply that they are not, they are just private. At the risk of your life you could try telling them that you hear that they are useless in bed but that everyone is too scared of them to tell them so. Perhaps this last option is best done by phone, preferably long distance!

4

Gemini–Sagittarius

'What about...' or 'Let's try...' or 'Why don't we...'

Bedroom etiquette

Both of these signs thrive on the essence of communication whether that communication is Geminian as in verbal or intellectual or Sagittarian as in philosophical and meaningful. They both pride themselves on their adaptability and their capacity to be flexible with a willing openness to trying anything new at least once. These two wanderers have the concept of communication in common. The good ones of each sign value their partners not for what they look like or what they earn but primarily for what is between their ears and the way that they communicate and intellectualise with each other whilst the lesser evolved ones twitter endlessly about nothing in general.

Geminis, with their well-known communication skills, will try anything in the bedroom as long as there is an oral/visual content. Talk to them in a foreign accent, wear your hair in a different style or express yourself in a constantly changing way. Wear masks, pretend to be a stranger. They like variety and whilst only the lower evolved Geminis actually make that variety physical, they all like the idea of the partner playing different roles in the bedroom. They chop and change a lot which makes it difficult for others to safely categorise them. They can believe one thing one day and the opposite the next, which leads to charges of being a hypocrite although perhaps chameleon is more appropriate. Sometimes it is hard to shut these budgerigars of the zodiac up, so keep their mouths occupied. Give them something to eat, or at least lick. Then they concentrate more fully on the matter in hand, which is often you. Sometimes it is only when the mouth is busy with something other than talking that they remember that they inhabit a physical body. They are wide open to any new experience as long as it doesn't inhibit their movement so they certainly don't do bondage and they even have difficulty with long lasting cuddles. Long drawn out silences or deep psychological and existential discussions in the bedroom are a real turn-off for these light-hearted chatterers. They like it light, active, talkative, mobile, interesting and fun.

Saggies like it communicative too but they also like it deep. They don't twitter so much as search for ultimate meaning in everything around them. Sex in itself can be seen as a fun function, something that provokes a concentrated doorway into the deeper, more vital areas of the higher self. If you really want to impress them, educate them both verbally and physically in the exotic and erotic experiences that you have learnt whilst travelling in distant lands. Teach them Tantra with didge music on in the background.

At the same time don't get too erudite. To a large degree subtlety and tact are wasted on them, they prefer the direct approach. Simple sounds insulting yet it works for them. The sensible Sagittarians know that if you always tell the truth you never have to remember what you have said. They all love a good bedtime story, as long as it has an element of adventure in it. Rub your hands up and down their spine as much as you can, it kind of grounds them. Like Gemini they can get so caught up in abstract and philosophy that they can forget to nurture and nourish the physical. They like the unusual and the interesting and anything with a foreign twist to it is manna from heaven. All Sagittarians at some time in their life go through a phase where they want to have sex in nature because it makes them feel more ethnic (very important Sagittarius word there). Environment is perhaps more important to them in sexual etiquette than any other sign. If they are not stimulated by the décor or the ambience of your place, you are off to a bad start.

How to enjoy food

Neither Gemini or Sagittarius are seen as gourmet aficionados, both seeing food as a supply of nutrients and energy to reach the parts of the body that other things don't reach. The difference between them is quite simple in that Gemini likes small mouthfuls whilst Sagittarius likes them big. In fact, Sagittarius likes everything big, whereas Gemini likes bite sized chunks using the philosophy that a little bit of everything is better than a lot of one or two things. In the long run they both prefer giggling and fumbling as opposed to eating in the bedroom, food is seen as an optional extra which can be taken or left. If food does enter their sex lives it won't be heavy and cumbersome, it will be light and easily eaten as well as quickly digested. Neither of them likes to go to bed on a full stomach, they like to keep their agility and mobility in tip-top condition.

Gemini and food? They haven't got time to eat, they have got a world to talk to and organise don't you know? Actually they do eat in the bedroom but primarily there are two conditions. Firstly, it has got to be light finger food that can be chewed and swallowed at the same time as talking because they can't let something as mundane as eating get in the way of important communication. Secondly, they like brain foods like nuts, dried fruit, seed bars and anything with lots of omega oils in it. Fast and slippery foods like bananas and yoghurt soothe the mind and lubricate the throat so are always welcome in the boudoir. They like to enjoy food fast. Long drawn out meals are seen as an unnecessary preamble to the far more important delights awaiting them in the bedroom.

Suck it and see is the Sagittarian motto as far as food is concerned at least in a sensual/sexual context. What they don't do is anything mundane and boring, they really are not your meat, potatoes and two vegetable person. What they do like is anything exotic preferably from far distant and foreign shores. Jalapeño peppers, anything spicy or hot or something novel and original. They are not the most subtle of diners and in the bedroom food is seen as an accessory instead of a necessity, sometimes even being seen as a distraction from the matter in hand. There is a fascination with chocolate in all of its different forms and applications. More than a mouthful at any one time is seen as extravagance but the quantity of successive mouthfuls is quite important. They don't mind fasting if it is for a spiritual purpose but they still like to know that they have got food in the cupboard.

Location, location

The average Saggie (if there is such a thing) isn't too bothered by degrees of aestheticism as long as there is a modicum of comfort. The ambience of the location is sometimes less important than the rusticness of it. A barn often features highly on their location wish list as does a forest, a cornfield, a deserted and sunlit beach or anywhere in the open air. They are not averse to a romp in the mud either, sex is perhaps the one thing that regularly grounds Sagittarius so for them to do it in contact with Mother Nature in whatever her shape or form is highly pleasurable. If you wish to bring out the sensuality of these dreamy and inspired travellers take them somewhere with a big view. They like to see the big picture. Of course, perhaps the ideal situation for them would be in a spacecraft with the spinning Earth visible through the windows.

Similarly, Geminis are also not too concerned with the delicacies and niceties of the physical location. They prefer an environment that can best be described as 'busy'. Music in the background, wind in the air, lots of different colours, outdoors or indoors, it doesn't matter as long as there is stimulation and not just at the physical level. To call them cluttered is a little unfair; they all like their personal environment to have a degree of verbal and aural stimulus. Remember that as far as Geminis are concerned the biggest sex organ is the one between the ears and that words, whether sweet nothings or factual information, create an energy field in themselves. These Janus worshippers pride themselves on their adaptability. Anywhere will do if the urge hits them suddenly and comfort comes second to the immediacy of the moment. When they want it, they want it now.

How to pamper them

How to pamper a Gemini? These connoisseurs of the spoken word enjoy anything that stretches their mind or gives them another string to their bow. Sweet nothings whispered in their ears, a lot of shoulder and neck massages, pleasant aromas, anything sensual that brings in an environment to help them switch off their non-stop verbal diarrhoea. All of these things have one common root, they all help them relax.

Getting a Gemini to relax is not an easy thing to do, it is something that takes them out of the normal and safe logical and rational environment that they live their lives in. Over a period of time this environment can become so frenetic that they can blow a fuse and the more they try to think or talk their way out of their problems the more complex those problems become.

To create an ambience of relaxation around them involves non-verbal therapy, something which is very hard for them to adjust to but which in time can really help them focus and centre themselves. They can be notoriously difficult to keep happy as they seemingly crave constant stimulation, occasionally living up to their reputation of having the attention span of a budgerigar but all Geminis love to be told that they are wanted and needed and that their mental and verbal input is important to those around them.

Sagittarius is much easier to please in a simple kind of way. They can happily spend hours poring over travel brochures and magazines, science fiction novels, the occasional philosophical or religious tract, anything that takes them out of what they can see as their normal humdrum day-to-day life. They crave excitement and anyone who can bring this to them automatically goes to the top of the list of close friends. It's much easier to pamper them when they are in some exotic location, preferably a long way from home. Whilst they can never completely relax (there is always something somewhere new to see or learn!), they do practice hard.

Sagittarians like the simple life and will run a mile from anything or anyone who represents complications, simple is not a rude word as far as they are concerned, it is a fact of life. They work on the principle that the shortest distance between two points is a straight line. Anything exotic, futuristic, fun and uncomplicated will automatically appeal to these travellers of the zodiac, especially if it is something that is out of the ordinary and brings a sense of adventure into their lives.

Favourite fantasies

Geminian fantasies can be varied, as befits their nature. They are truly the experimenters of the zodiac and really will try anything once, as long as it doesn't involve them being restricted or limited in any way. Unlike their Sagittarian cousins they are not hot on travelling far away unless they can have communications with home at the drop of a button. Nevertheless, they like to feel as though the world is at their fingertips. They like their partners to pretend to be different people, to wear disguises, to speak in different accents or to behave as though they have different personalities. It's not that they are schizophrenic or bi-polar but they do like the idea of variation, even if the act itself normally goes beyond their remit.

All Geminis like their romantic and sexual potentials to be fully explored, there is nothing boring about these original thinkers. They will jump into bed, on a blanket or onto the sofa at anytime and anywhere, they will assume any position (at least once!) and they will always be in the frame of mind for tickling and laughing. Not for nothing are these people known as the wrigglepusses of the zodiac. Remember that for them the biggest sex organ is the one between the ears, so keep them stimulated mentally and they will always be loyal and true. As long as they are mentally stimulated they have an enormous capacity to 'make do'.

In a completely different world Sagittarius doesn't really have that much consideration for fantasy as he\she spends much of their time in a fantasy world anyway, always dreaming of being whisked away to foreign shores or finding a rich prince/princess who will make their dreams come true. Saggies live much of their time in a dream world where they don't have to cope with the reality and daily hardships of the modern world. They long to be cooped up with their partner in a tree house in the jungle with the nearest human miles away so that they can let themselves go and truly be themselves. They secretly desire to be swept away by some well-built, muscular and bronzed barbarian of either gender (I'm convinced that the Valkyries are a Sagittarian construct) who will take them to the heights of physical passion. They like to be chased (not chaste!) because half the fun of the hunt lies in the being caught as far as they are concerned.

Sagittarians are known for their broadmindedness in most situations and can adapt willingly to whatever is going on around them. For some obscure reason they all want to try having sex off of the ground whether it be in outer space or just up a tree. I guess it's the idea of being off planet that turns them on so much. In the long run their greatest desire is to have fun, they all work on the principle that a good laugh is the best relaxant in the bedroom.

What they really, really want

Neither of these signs could be accused of being purist, they both have an amazing capacity to make do and can chop and change at a moment's notice. These two signs are the hardest to please, simply because much of the time they don't know what they really want!

Ask a Gemini what it is that they really want if you want but make sure you have a good capacity recording device to hand and it is switched on. These paradoxes of reason have lists that run for miles and miles in many different directions with sections of those lists being promoted to urgency seemingly at a whim. The secret to giving them what they want is actually quite simple; it just takes a leap in the dark. You have to make and take actions, giving them a break from the decision-making process. This gives them the freedom to just go with the flow instead of orchestrate it, although it also gives them something to disagree with if they don't like what you have done. What they really want is to share the initiatory approach, someone intelligent to be with whom they can follow as much as lead and lots of different forms of oral expression, especially in between the sheets.

As with Gemini if you ask a Sagittarian what they really want you'd best be prepared for a wait before you get to the final answer. Not because of all the details but because of the ethics, the philosophical sides of their desires, the moral issues connected with their wants and whether or not their reasons for wanting what they want stand up to examination in the cold light of day. No one else can give a Saggie what they can only find within themselves but you can help by making them laugh both at themselves and the world. What they really want is a clear path forward, a committed direction in life that they don't have to think about and for life to be simple. In theory easy, yes?

What to watch out for

When dealing with Gemini remember that you are dealing with an agent of Janus the two-faced one. This is not to imply hypocrisy but is to suggest a chameleon-like ability that can adapt to any situation at a moment's notice. They can always see and defend both sides of an argument with anyone and the skilled ones can do it with themselves and others at the same time. They can be contrary whilst defying anyone else to be anything but the truth. Geminian eyes sometimes roll from side to side and they often hop from foot to foot. It is not indecision that plagues them as much as the variety of choices and this can make them appear flustered. They have been known at their worst to stop mid-sex to ask about the shopping list, or whether there is enough petrol in the car. That damn overactive brain again...

A glazed, faraway look with a detached and impersonal side to the communication makes it difficult to get any type of clear decision from Sagittarius. These wanderers of the zodiac have difficulty totally attaching themselves to any current point in space and time because the future can sometimes take precedence over the present. The time to be worried is when they irradiate you with an almost zealot-like look and say with utmost conviction, "Yes I will, I promise!" At this point, unless they are one of the very few Saggies who have learnt the reality about commitment, you might start to question their sanity.

Both of these signs are surprisingly flexible about issues of truth and honesty. That is not to impugn them as to the veracity of their content but it is to suggest that they have a degree of adaptability and tolerance in their mental and verbal outpourings. Gemini and Sagittarius have an element of trickster about them and one should never take them as they appear to be at any given time.

How to wind them up

To wind up a Sagittarian is simple, just point out the lack of realism in their philosophies and plans. Laugh more than they do, travel more than them, wear longer and baggier sweaters, do everything bigger and better and louder than them. If you really want to upset them, the best swear word is the dreaded 'c' word commitment, although the word responsibility has also been known to induce an attack of the cold sweats more than once. Tell them that they lack belief or faith and worst of all suggest that their sense of humour is crass.

With Gemini, curtail their freedom. Corner them at parties so that they can't move about and circulate and bore them to death with long monologues about your personal problems. Give them big intimate hugs and then don't let go. Geminis like hugging for three or four seconds. They can't stand being constrained. Even the baby Geminis will crawl to the edge of the playpen and try to climb out. Suggest that they are discriminate and when they disagree add argumentativeness to the list.

5

Cancer–Capricorn

Snuggle, nestle, grunt and groan…

Bedroom etiquette

Cancerians are such a neurotic bunch much of the time it's a miracle that they even know where the bedroom is, let alone its potential uses (and before we go any further at all remember that I'm one of you!). To them the bedroom represents the womb-like centre of nurturing, where they are at both their most vulnerable and their most sensual. It is where in the long run the practice of cuddling and hugging is at least as intimate as other more sexual forms of expression. The secret way to their heart is to give them lots of reassuring body contact.

More than any other sign of the zodiac Cancer understands the real meaning of the word tactile; touch is seen by them as being the most reassuring of feelings. Of course, the opposite way of relating to Cancerian tactility in the bedroom is to observe their crab-like tenacity. Once you are in the crab's claws you had best prepare for extensive body contact! Notoriously shy but when they do finally bolster themselves and find the courage to come out of their shells and tell you what they feel, you will be amazed at how sensual these water babies really are. They all go for the spoon position for some strange reason and are willing to try anything if they feel loved enough.

Remember that at the end of the line they are real home lovers and more than any other sign they know the difference between house and home, house being where you live but home being where you belong.

Capricorns are real animals in the bedroom in that they really like to get in there in a fertile way that exudes the more basic forms of lust and sensuality or else they do the opposite typical Capricorn thing of being sexually functional in ways that satisfy but little else. Given the wrong circumstances Capricorn will retreat into shyness and reserve even to the point of getting undressed in the dark and treating sex as something that is necessary but that's as far as it goes. They can be more concerned with getting it right than they are with identifying with the feel and the flow of the times, to the point of alienating themselves from their body.

At the same time Capricorns can switch, suddenly identify with their more animalistic nature and then there is no stopping them. They like nothing more than getting dirty and earthy and in the dark underneath the quilt cover they like nothing more than to really get in close to their partner. For some strange reason known only to other Capricorns they all like burying their faces in their partners' armpits and nuzzling their way into olfactory heaven whilst at the same time enjoying all the other sides of physical intimacy. At the end of the day etiquette in the bedroom goes beyond much of Capricorn's radar in that they either do what needs to be done or they get in touch with their inner animal and either way subtlety is something that comes second.

How to enjoy food

I'm pretty sure that it was a Cancerian that invented yoghurt. All crabs seem attracted to cold, thick, slippery and tasty yoghurt, especially if a hot body lies just underneath. Anything creamy is a real turn on if eaten to effect, with sweet being an optional extra hence the majority of them having a fetish for succulent exotic fruit. They all like cheese, it is something that's imprinted on their DNA and gives them their cholesterol hit and also stops some of them becoming vegan. In the bedroom they enjoy anything that is a combination of sensuality and taste, using warm honey or ice-cold strawberries in strategic places for example and they don't mind getting sticky. Food can be the passport to intimacy and the land of slippery heaven for these most sensuous of signs. If you really want to worm your way into your partner's affections, bring them breakfast in bed and then jump on them. In the evening, they perform best hungry with a snack afterwards. In the morning, it's the other way round.

Goats on the other hand really go for the structured feasts with lots of roast potatoes, solid stodge and any savoury flavouring. It has to be hot and ideally it has to be on time and at an affordable price as well, so to them it's just food with the organic and/or whole food option being only a bonus. Sometimes they neglect desserts because they don't feel they deserve them. The idea of food in the bedroom can be quite a distraction to these methodical souls, their philosophy is that biscuit crumbs are just a distraction and anything yucky just has to be rinsed off afterwards and then there is the washing. As one of my Capricorn friends put it to me recently, "Food and sex? Where do you put the gravy?" Of course there is the other option, being that if you want to seduce a Capricorn, tempt them into the bedroom with the offer of not only a hot body but a hot meal too.

Location, location

Cancer relates strongly to the pull and the light of the Moon so their desire for intimacy and shelter as opposed to being 'out there' is like the tides being up and down over the period of a month. Half the time they crave the darkness and the safe warmth of the bedroom in their own personal grotto, secure with partner in the primal state ensconced in feeling and emotion. The other half of the time they are more than content to be out there, anywhere... They like water. Saunas, swimming pools, the beach, showers and baths, jacuzzies particularly, they all like being in some type of moving water in amorous situations. The more adventurous will happily spend romantic interludes in caves merrily potholing away whilst a lot of them secretly fantasise about a tent in the desert, a cabin deep in the forest or even an igloo in the tundra. The secret with Cancer and location is not so much where they go to sleep and wake up but how they wake up, who they wake up with and how the first few minutes go.

Capricorns on the other hand have a great deal of variation in their dreams of location. Bearing in mind that most of them have a secret fantasy of being constrained to some degree, they don't mind where they are as long as there are boundaries. The women are the ones who wear tight corsets and suspenders and dream of being chased half naked through the woods, whilst the men normally wear garters or tight belts and are often to be found in proximity to anything that can be used for spanking. Deserted forests with their lovers bring out the earthier and basic side of their desire whilst fetish clubs and dungeons bring out their more depraved potentials but in either case the location is only the backdrop for the potential that can occur. It probably won't happen but they like to feel that it could, hence their desire to have either total control or total surrender over their location for erotic dalliances.

How to pamper them

It is said in old lore that the way to a Cancer's heart is through their stomach and this is based on fact to an extent. Even more than chocolate and ice cream though, they like fruit. They run on fine food but do ration them as many find it easy to put on weight as they enter middle age. Put your arm around their shoulders regularly and remind them that they are more popular and that they are wanted more than they give themselves credit for. Make them feel valued. They all like massage of various types although they profess to not needing or even wanting it and react favourably to anything concerning their health and diet. The best thing anyone can do for them is to make them feel not only wanted and valued but also safe and secure and even the most macho of Cancerians will gradually open up more and more to basic hugs and cuddles as they get older. Breakfast in bed is a sure-fire winner, every time. Remember that above all else, Cancerians need to be smiled at and loved first thing in the morning. It makes life easier for everyone.

I know that it is a cliché but Capricorns really do like antiques. They enjoy the company of people older than themselves regardless of age. Anything that has antiquity as much as value, especially if older than they are, gives them a sense of both hope and security. They like mementos of their youth, the more understated the better. They don't do flamboyance although if you are strong and determined enough to get through their reserve you will find that they actually like quality luxury, especially if it is of the vintage type. Buy them old whisky or 1960s saucy movies, or if you really want to make them happy buy them a grandfather clock or tickets to a show with a twenty-year track record. Anything will do if it has class and preferably a pedigree because here one finds the most prized of Capricorn values, that of continuity and consistency over a period of time.

Favourite fantasies

There is a drippy side to every Cancerian, a little bit that still dreams of prince and princesses and the kind of dewy-eyed romanticism that really belongs in Disney. They all want to own a hotel where they can live in the penthouse with a swimming pool. Rarely do Cancerians groan out loud but if you can get them to do this either in a sexual or a culinary way (or better still, a combination of both) you know that you are on a winner by appealing to their senses, primarily touch and taste but also sight, sound and speech. They love to be stroked, oiled, touched, teased, occasionally fed off of and generally adored in as many physical ways as feasible at the time. At the same time, they also occasionally revel in taking the role of worshipper or advocate of their partner as they are not so self-centred that they neglect others.

Capricorns on the other hand are the epitome of extremes as far as self-centredness goes. They like to be the total centre of attention, being worshipped, adored, stroked, loved and admired to the fullness of potential or else they like to be firmly in the role of worshipper and disciple. They secretly dream of being dominated or dominating, the idea of being all powerful or powerless appeals to the side of them that enjoys constraints whether in their clothing or in other more personal and secretive ways. Capricorns truly believe that they are the best equipped to set the moral standards for everyone else and are astonished when others disagree with their view from upon high. Delusions of grandeur and power normally keep these soft-centred but hard-edged people content and act as a buffer to the harshness of the outside and sometimes more real world.

What they really, really want

In a nutshell, Capricorns want power. Not so much power over anyone or anything but power in their situations. Unfortunately, the lesser evolved Capricorn will think that the only way for them to have power is to be in control and this can lead to all types of problems in their drive to what they see as safety and others see as authority. They really want to feel solid and structured and know that their sex life is going to be not so much conventional and safe as it is semi predictable and mildly kinky. They want only the best, whatever it is. They all need lots of massage but also need to be forced into it so I guess that a nine-month course of tantric massage practice would combine the sensual and the tactile in a way that brings them the greatest and best form of power manifestation, that of power within.

Cancers start with power from within and graduates to extending that power into the outside world as they age in terms of home, safety, family and a sense of continuity that brings emotional stability. In terms of physical things that they actually want, the content itself doesn't matter, it is the way that it is presented and decorated that makes Cancerians feel the most valued and wanted by their community. They want to feel as though they are an integral part of everything that's going on and that they belong because this makes them feel secure. Being wanted is like a kind of psychic teddy bear or hot water bottle. Similar to Capricorn you know that your Cancerian bed buddy is feeling safe with you when they start getting in really tight and begin snuggling into all available nooks and crannies.

What to watch out for

With Cancer it really does what it says on the tin. Their famous capacity for moodiness can show up at any time, in any circumstances and with anyone. They can easily switch moods especially first thing in the morning in a way that can catch others by surprise. The sensible option is to leave them alone for a time and let them work it out for themselves. It normally takes about five minutes but they need to be alone to do it. They are protective of their space so enter it with respect and this means take your shoes off at the door, only enter their bed if you are clean and presentable and be aware of their need for fairly constant reassurance and comfort. In some cases it is unfortunately true that with some Cancerians, particularly the men, there can be a need to gently and slowly prise them free of attachment to the mother, normally best done by living more than an hour's drive away from the in-laws.

With Capricorn it is often the image of the father that is seen as the overriding iconic figure that needs to be superseded in order for quality relationships to develop, although this is often truer in Capricorn women than it is in the men. They can suddenly turn the charm on or off and when you feel that you are being played with it is perhaps time to start planning an exit strategy whilst you can. If they suddenly give you the stone-cold treatment you know you are in trouble. This is why Capricorns like climbing cliffs, the granite-like unyielding appearance hides a multitude of feelings and sins but they are not going to let you anywhere near this unless they really trust you, so deal with them honourably and all will be well.

How to wind them up

With Capricorn's sense of propriety and dignity the last thing they want to do is be seen as emotional, affectionate or demonstrative, especially in public. They are not even that good at holding hands in public unless they have been with you for seven years. So get them to describe their feelings to you in crowded train stations or find other ways of embarrassing them in public because they are not good at dealing with the more sensual stuff in the outside world. Once their structures dissolve they become all gooey and there is nothing more pitiful than a boundary-less Capricorn. It helps to remind them occasionally of their lowly position in the hierarchical chain and if you really want to offend them it can sometimes be done by comparing them to their father. Their organising ability is legendary so you do everything and insist that they sit down and put their feet up whilst you do everything around them, it will drive them nuts. These are people who need a week's practise on how to go on holiday.

Cancerians are even easier to wind up, especially the more traditional members of their clan. Whether they like it or not they are all emotionally tied to the apron strings and any criticism of their mother will be met with the emotional equivalent of world war three. Remember that their mothers are sacrosanct and above criticism and all will be well. Although nearly as bad is the idea of criticising their kitchens, because Cancerians work on the principle that a healthy and full stomach is the one necessity for a good lifestyle. Of course, the Cancerian attachment to home is legendary. The easiest way to get on their wrong side is to warn them that their house is about to go through compulsory purchase because a motorway is coming through their back yard, tomorrow. The men lose their hair and get a paunch as they age whilst the women just become more and more maternal in a community type of way, so referring to them as 'gramps' or 'grandma' in any situation is going to lose you friends quickly as well.

6

Leo–Aquarius

The experience of fun...

Bedroom etiquette

Every sign of the zodiac has their favourite space in the home but without a doubt Leo's space is the bedroom. This is the area where you can be sure that they are going to pull out all the stops to ensure that the bedroom is a place of luxury, opulence and elegance, pleasure, sumptuous décor, anything that in their eyes epitomises true style and comfort. They like it lush with rugs and quilts and cushions everywhere so they can sprawl and let their tummy be tickled. The bedroom is their domain and watch out anyone who attempts to move in without their permission. Outside of the bedroom Leo is the perfect person. Inside the bedroom they are the world's biggest porn star, at least in their eyes.

The two most important things outside of the bed itself are the en-suite bathroom (absolutely essential), ideally one per person and of course a deep loose pile shag rug beside the bed to curl those claws into when you step out of the imperial domain that is the regal bed. The bed itself is pivotal. There has to be a hard mattress, a large bed frame for lounging and stretching and large pillows. Ideally, the bed would be a four-poster with velvet curtains and a golden bedspread, looking out the window to sunrise over the cliff tops. Even in the smallest of apartments the Leo bedroom will be sacrosanct.

In the bed itself Leo likes to be lord and master or lady and mistress of all they control, often taking a more dominant role. Other times the complete opposite is evident and some Leos just like to be gently stroked and slowly led to the Promised Land as much as rushed there in a hurry. Remind them how good they are and how much they mean to you because there is nothing quite as sad as a Leo with nothing to feel proud about.

Whereas to an Aquarian the style, décor or setting of the bedroom has less significance, indeed most of them don't notice and don't even care. Remember that to many Aquarians sex is either a functional thing or something that comes upon you only at certain times. You have to take into account that perhaps the first word that comes up when you think of Aquarius and the bedroom is different, closely followed by experimental. These are the people who prefer to take risks, doing it in car parks, cornfields or in elevator shafts, anywhere out of the norm and convention. The location itself isn't so important; it's the adventure and the thrill of the unusual that does it for them. However they make the effort, it will be something with a difference and it should be fun.

Strangely enough, these people are champion kissers. Perhaps it's the idea of sharing that degree of intimacy that helps them remember that they live in a sexual body but once they get it hardwired into their system they then develop the ideas into a philosophy that could be broadly categorized as 'anything goes'. It's not that they are radical or free with sex but they don't like to be limited or restricted in their desires and wouldn't dream of putting any limitations on others. If you give them the freedom they crave they will never abuse it. If you put boundaries on them, they will only break them. Aquarians generally like sex as it helps them stay in contact with both themselves and the rest of the human race.

How to enjoy food

As with everything Leos only do the best. They know the best restaurants and eateries, the most exclusive and the best bargains and they love to show off so let them take you out or even better let them cook for you. It's with food that the really childish side of mature Leo can suddenly arise so remember to compliment them on their taste. If you are cooking for them make it look good, quality presentation cheers them up and makes them feel good. They like their eggs sunny side up and if you are going to dare to enter the lair of the bedroom then bring only the ripest fruits and most succulent offerings to prepare your way. It's not really that important what the food itself is, it is the quality and the way in which it is offered that works for these connoisseurs of class. Every so often they need to be custard pied, just to remind them of their own humility.

Whereas Aquarians and food? Some see it as the fuel that empowers the system whilst others are real epicures. There is the more communal side of food that says that they prefer to live in cafes and restaurants as opposed to cooking regularly and when they do cook it's never quite conventional or routine. As with everything, there is a basic functional approach to food in that Aquarians will see food as the thing that keeps the body healthy and therefore the lifestyle working and the more humane amongst them will eat ethically. If you broach the subject of food in the bedroom, half of them will look at you with one of those 'are you mad?' stares before shaking their head and muttering something unintelligible, whilst the rest will stare at you for a second and then rush off to the organic supermarket, returning with all types of fresh foodstuff and a very fertile mind and imagination. That's it with Aquarians and food. You never know what you are going to get unless you try.

Location, location

As with most things Leonine, it is not the physical location that attracts them as much as the style, the splendour and the presentation that counts. They like large rooms where they can pace up and down or sprawl luxuriously on the chaise longue and they like space to roam. Always with Leo, anywhere with sunshine is going to be a relatively safe bet. These ardent sun worshippers prefer the feel of the sun on their skin almost as much as they do the latest styles and it doesn't matter if it's the desert or the beach as long as the sunshine is around. It increases their passion and libido, makes their hair bounce more and does their well-being the world of good. There needs to be a patio and ideally a swimming pool for lounging around and of course partner/staff to fill the wine glass. Run to where the hot weather is and give them half a chance and these sun worshippers will follow you anywhere.

Aquarius on the other hand isn't given to locations of indolence, complacency or luxury. Aquarius doesn't care if it is a caravan in the woods, a hut in the mountains, a convenience hotel or the Hawaiian beach as long as it's not mundane and boring. Aquarius will go to the ends of the earth for variation, they are the type of person who will take you to remote locations and then instigate kinky outdoor sex or they will be content to let you make all the running, being fascinated to see where someone else would like to take them. Given the choice the best sex would probably be in a yurt in the Gobi Desert or in a tree house somewhere in the jungle or anywhere where they could be different, because this is what secretly powers their sex drive: the spontaneity and unpredictability is the key to their passion.

How to pamper them

There are two basic ways to pamper and treat your 'average' Aquarian if there is such a thing. The one way that is always guaranteed success is to put them in touch with the latest craze, fad, fashion etc. just so that they can go through it and come out the other side way ahead of their time in about five minutes flat. They like to be aware of what's going on so that they can be ahead of their contemporaries so buy them lots of little gizmos and gadgets that remind them that they are living in a technological society based in the twenty-first century and that they are ambassadors to the future for the rest of us.

If you need evidence of this look at their passion for the odd, new and quirky, futuristic and the downright weird. Alternatively there is a more hands-on and direct approach based around getting Aquarius more in touch with their physical side. Buy them sex toys or rude DVDs for when you are not with them, or buy them memberships for the gym. They like to feel safe in their relationships but also need their freedom so get them a season ticket for the railways or rent the pair of you a remote log cabin in the mountains for a week where you can just play and pamper with each other. They have a childish delight in exploring other people's bodies as much as their mind and when they are in the right mood be sure that the only thing they really want is you.

In a similar way to Aquarius, Leo can sometimes take it or leave it as far as sex goes. If sex and its accompanying pleasures aren't to the Leo's taste or preference they can become as dispassionate as cold steel. If you want to get them to open up to you then the first thing that you do is be nice to their body. They love the tactility of sex so fondle, touch, stroke, hug, lick and kiss everywhere you can. Get them the best (and the classiest, don't forget that) organic body cream, gel or moisturiser. Treat their body as a temple to pray at and be grateful for the honour. Remember though that servility is contemptible in these proud warrior's eyes so don't ever, ever patronise them. If you need to tell them about their body odour do so whilst also complimenting them on their skin texture and physical tone.

Then there are the mirrors. They all hate to be seen preening themselves, too much inverse snobbery but secretly they would all love to have mirror lined bedrooms. It is their reflection into the world that is their secret fetish so take them places where they can be seen because there is no one quite like Leo for flaunting their fabulousness. Anything that encourages them to put on a show helps them manifest their flamboyance and they all fulfil stereotypical Leo tradition here in that when they are out on the world stage they always look good in gold or red. If all else fails, put an arm around them and stroke their hair or their belly because every cat likes to have its tummy tickled or its mane brushed.

Favourite fantasies

Leo likes to think of itself as bounding across the veldt chasing prey, fully resplendent when at its prime and able to provide and protect the other members of its pride. They like to see themselves as noble, proud people. They brush their hair back when in their power, gazing haughtily over their domain and they wish their subjects to worship them. They want to be adored and loved but remember that in their fantasies you play a pivotal role, your image to the outside world plays a big role in Leo's fantasy life. To them you are sometimes a projection of themselves. Regardless of gender, they all secretly want a harem. Not to use (well – perhaps occasionally) but just so that it's there should they want to. Whilst they can't be bothered about the details of other people's lives, they like to retain a degree of influence over their partner's lives as it makes them feel a little safer if they can predict things.

It's the opposite for Aquarius. Whilst Leo is content to deal with things at the external and sensual level, Aquarius lives their fantasy life almost exclusively internally, finding it surprising that other people have similar tastes and styles as them. They all secretly believe that they are the reincarnation of an old temple priest from Atlantis and their dream lives are often little to do with current times or situations, preferring instead to be in the long distant past or else some techno-cyborg future where everything is somehow a lot more simple. No matter how normal or different, strange or conventional the Aquarian fantasies are they will not be interested in doing them with or in the world in terms of group. Here the famed Aquarian community principle fades into the background because when it comes to personal fantasy they like to be alone or else just with partner(s). They are somewhat exclusive in that they don't go out on a Friday night because that's when the common people go out.

What they really, really want

These two signs really do contradict and oppose each other. Sometimes there are similarities between opposites but not in this case. Leo will want to be in, affect and play with the outside world whilst at the same time knowing that it is only playing and interacting whilst Aquarius will operate effectively and functionally in terms of dealing with most other people and environments but the real work will be going on inside as they try and balance themselves with what they see as the madness of the outside world.

Aquarius sometimes wants nothing more than to be left alone. Even in the context of a fully functional and healthy long-term relationship they will still occasionally scream at the world to "Just leave me alone!" Yet once they have spent just a little time alone they start to feel out of sorts and as a result come back to their community for further stimulation and reminders that they live in a social society where they have an important role to play. They want their life to be sane and to an extent safe as well as relatively stable.

Whilst they are always up for seeing things in a new light it can be difficult for them to exit long prepared grooves of pattern because they do get entrenched as they get older, increasingly valuing stability and security above all else. If that means being alone then so be it although this is bottom of the list for preferred options. Aquarius wants to feel safe in its community regardless of number because as they age so they realise that despite the individuality and eccentricity of youth they need people to bounce off of.

Make them feel welcome and wanted and they will be the most loyal of friends. They can get a bit overly attached so send them off into the wilds every so often; it puts them in touch with their humanity and gets them out of a rut.

Whereas Leo is the complete opposite, thriving on attention, group and community and wouldn't consider going off on their own in most circumstances unless it was to eat in private. What they all really want is to be secretly adored and admired, from afar or up close, it doesn't matter. They want the security of family, especially the younger members around them, they can easily grow into being the family patriarch or matriarch. They really want something to show off about and often this means you, so dress up if you are going out with them and remember that you are an extension of them when you are in the outside world. The world does revolve around them or at least that's how they see it and even the more reticent ones do expect you to know when they enter the room. So laugh at their jokes, compliment them on their hairstyle and make them aware of how highly you regard them then they will never leave.

What to watch out for

Leos can be really disdainful; once they turn off of you, they turn off for life. There is the famous Leo pride to be aware of although there are two different versions of it. The higher Leos will have pride in their achievements, their projects, their partners and their children (the lion's pride). Pride is a virtue, something to be earned and worked for. The other side of the same coin is arrogance, conceit and vanity, the kind of false pride that only the lower type of superficial Leos ascribe to. They can have a kind of infuriating smugness about them where they don't even have to try to convince either themselves or the outside world that they are the best, whether it's the workplace or the bedroom, because they simply know it. The Sun does shine out of this playful person but every so often they need to remember that the applause needs to be earned and deserved and not taken for granted otherwise they become the ruler without a tribe.

Aquarius also has a strange attitude towards lower mortals. They sometimes feel so out of touch with other humans that they can retreat onto their own high lofty perch and watch from a higher place where the emotional attachments aren't quite so strong. They can have a capacity for treating others like cogs in the machine and need to be reminded every so often that they need to eat, breathe, cuddle and do other things that humans do. Sometimes when they appear to turn off sexually they only do so physically. They often retreat into self-loving as they are the only ones that understand themselves, at least at certain levels. Whilst their willingness to experiment is the sign of a fertile mind, don't let them stray too far out into the sexual wilderness because sometimes it's hard for them to find their way back, which is why a lot of celibates of all types are more Aquarian than any other sign. Keep them in touch, preferably with you but at least with themselves.

How to wind them up

Leos are so seemingly invulnerable that they take anything on the chin, everything deflects off of them, but they do have a few weak points. Traditionally they all have an inordinate amount of pride in their appearance, so jokes or suggestions about the hairstyle are generally dangerous territory and comments about their dress sense or fashion style will always go down like a lead balloon. They consider their taste and judgement to be the epitome of style, so comments otherwise will be frowned upon. All of these things fade into the background compared to the one real weak point in Leo's life, this being their ugly children. After all, the lion's pride and all that...

Aquarians, on the surface at least, are far less likely to bite than your average Leo because they do such a good job of seeming detached that it's as though words go in one ear and out the other. They do value their freedom so much that it is impossible for them to stick to a fixed and permanent schedule so insisting that they inform you of their regular plans and movements will definitely cramp their style. As will getting all personal and intimate in a tight and confined space unless it's their idea. Take them for granted. Accuse them of being cyborg walk-ins from Sirius C. Challenge their ideas of the future, accusing them of secretly being a hippy. Take away their crystals.

7

Virgo–Pisces

Making it flow with the go

Bedroom etiquette

Sometimes opposites attract and other times they really repel. Some of the interplay between Virgo and Pisces is highly complementary but as far as the bedroom goes that similarity is not that strong. In certain ways they are poles apart from each other particularly in terms of functionality, order and intuition but in other ways such as those of health, service, pain and suffering they do have a resonance with each other that is only perhaps matched elsewhere by the Taurus/Scorpio combination. With both signs sex is not just to be enjoyed, it is to be experienced, felt, worked and danced with in an instinctual and intuitive way incorporating both the mind and the body. Remember that they are opposites. Pisces will light the incense to create a more relaxed environment; Virgo will go and get the brush and dustpan.

As far as bedroom etiquette goes Virgo probably wrote the rule book. These are the kids who never get shouted at to tidy their bedroom. Watch them. The more obsessive they are about cleanliness and order in the bedroom the more there is likely to be some ghastly secret lurking under the floorboards, at the very least an ancient encrusted sock if not far worse. They all have something to hide about what they see as their inadequacies and because of this in the bedroom Virgo will go to great lengths to satisfy their partner. Once they start learning how to relax into things and not worry so much about performance they lighten up and become better lovers although they will always be trying to take you apart and put you back together again because that is what they do. One good thing with Virgo, through all the functionality and the effectiveness, is that at least you can be sure that the sheets will be relatively clean.

Pisces on the other hand are nothing like this. Firstly, the environment of the bedchamber is representative of their current state of mind so if it's untidy when you get in there you know what you are letting yourself in for. Secondly Pisces doesn't really care that much about things like functionality or performance. It just likes to float along in its own world at its own pace and in its own time knowing that by being flexible it will be able to adapt with whatever situation it finds itself in. Having said all of that Pisces is very partial indeed to a large en suite bathroom/steam room with a big jacuzzi. They are less concerned about the décor or the tidiness and more concerned about the ambience and the background music and atmosphere. They will go for the essences, oils and cushions and drapes and try to create an environment they can lose themselves in.

Both of these signs can lack boundaries in the bedroom and should not allow themselves to get too deeply involved in any type of extreme relationship pattern where they feel constantly undervalued. There can be an attraction to an almost S&M lifestyle and unless they are very good at setting and maintaining boundaries this shouldn't be followed too far. Sometimes it is the idea of pain, whether mental, verbal, emotional or even physical, that makes these people feel alive to a degree and this attraction to situations of service or duty for others can lead them into feelings of being degraded or undervalued. Remember you are a servant not a slave; you do things for others because you want to not because they want you to. As soon as you start to feel obliged or taken for granted it's time to walk.

How to enjoy food

Virgos enjoy food in a kind of regimented way. These are the people who arrange the things on their plate into separate piles, chew diligently and are concerned that they get their minerals and vitamins regularly. Often overly concerned about their digestive systems they go for the healthy option given the choice. As far as food in the bedroom goes, they will cautiously try anything once as long as a couple of basic rules are observed. Firstly, that after the whole gooey and yucky business is over there should be both a shower and a washing machine close to hand and that secondly there should be no crumbs. Not ever. The idea of crumbs in the bed is the Virgoan idea of hell so biscuits in bed with your lover are out of the question if they are a Virgo. If they are umming and ahing about taking food into the bedroom tell them that what you are going to eat off of them is both organic and free trade and that should tip the balance.

Pisces are fine with almost anything as far as food goes but the more sensitive of them will draw the line at anything slimy especially if it lives under the waves. They are good with most fish but generally don't do eels or shellfish and they certainly don't do any food at all which still has eyes. They are not that fond of boiled or steamed vegetables and prefer a lighter diet than stodgy. As far as the bedroom goes whilst any type of yoghurt, honey or other form of lubricant will gel well most Pisceans only see food as just another prop alongside the ambience, décor and music. To them it is the emotional and sensual content that is the real food of the soul. They all have one guilty secret as far as the bedchamber and culinary delights go. Bring them strawberries, cream and especially champagne in bed and they are yours if not for life then at least for the next few hours.

Location, location

It's obvious that all Pisceans tend to gravitate towards the seaside, yes? Actually this is one of those rare generalisations in astrology that work in that being next to moving bodies of water creates an energy of calm and serenity within these sensitive souls and they will become naturally more empathic and intuitive the closer they live to the sea or a flowing river or stream. To make them feel safe and secure install a tinkling fountain in the garden or even the living room because the background sound of water falling really helps them calm their minds. They can't relax in the throng of the crowd so if they live in the middle of a city there will be a real need every so often to get out of the madness into the natural world in order to download and here again the sea is the best medicine of all. The actual point where the water meets the shore is a magical spot where Pisceans can really find their peace and solace within themselves and then bring it back to the rest of us.

Whereas Virgo is a completely different kettle of fish and will always be looking to be industrious, wherever it is. A working holiday on a farm is far more preferable than lounging for a week on a beach because that represents idleness, something most Virgos aren't that good at dealing with either in themselves or in others. The sea dissolves the edges of their boundaries and it makes some of them a little nervous without quite knowing why whereas being in the open-air countryside in the heart of nature is something they all naturally gravitate towards as they age. Virgo needs a work room whether it's a little cubby hole under the stairs or a barn. It's somewhere to set their work tools out in order because then they feel that they are safe and they can really become more established and functional to the point of contentment, even happiness as they age.

The idea for both Virgo and Pisces in terms of location is to find a place without too many others in close proximity where you can be at one with both yourself and nature, a place where you can get your psychic space.

How to pamper them

The ideas of pampering and Virgo seem a rather odd combination at first as Virgo likes to be dutiful and attentive more than indulgent and wallowing. Break through that immaculate exterior and there is a sensitive internal side, one that craves attention and love. They all like to be fed; it makes them feel that people value them enough to fuel them, much as they do other machines of service. Create an environment of order and general tidiness around them so that they can relax knowing that everything is working and they don't have to fret or worry. Make sure that the larder and the fridge are full of wholesome good organic food and that the medicine cabinet containing all the essences and alternative treatments is not that far away. I know it sounds crass but what these mentally driven people really enjoy is space to be creative. A good jigsaw does wonders for mental relaxation.

The way to pamper Pisces is definitely through the body. As with Virgo, feeding them works, it grounds them and makes them feel wanted and valued but for Pisces there is a much better way of treating them and making them feel good and that's by laying your hands on their bodies. They all secretly crave the personal touch of another human being because it gives them a sense of solidity and groundedness so always remember to hug them. Offers of massage are normally gratefully received, it's as though the touch of another helps them integrate and consolidate themselves. True, they like times alone so that they can experience the more nebulous and respect for their space is always appreciated but do keep an eye on them from afar and sometimes bring them back into the real world again so that they can remember why they volunteered to come here.

Favourite fantasies

For Pisces, the ultimate fantasy is that of total surrender. Not surrender to any particular person, belief, experience or situation but surrender to the universal all, to dissolve boundaries of individuality and unite with the universe in a way that brings them into what they see as a state of completion. Obviously whilst they aspire to this the limitations of a three-dimensional body are a little difficult so compromises have to be made. Nevertheless, anything that takes them out of the mundane and physical is something that can be really attractive to these spiritual seekers. The danger here is not knowing your boundaries, which is why alcohol, narcotics and all other toxins should be moderated, but that warning aside the idea of melting warm chocolate-like into the embrace of the other is something that will always make them feel safe and protected whilst they are off exploring their own private dream worlds.

Whereas with Virgo the complete opposite applies, they like their fantasies to be grounded, down to earth and real and what's more this is one of the few signs that can actually make their fantasies real. There is a need for caution here because Virgo's tendency to try and establish control of situations as a safety mechanism can lead them into dominance or subjugation issues that can push deep primal buttons and needs to be expressed only in safe and stable situations. They have a defined purist philosophy. I guess this means that more Virgos are nudists than any other sign; certainly they work on a philosophy of 'this is me, warts and all, so take it or leave it'. Part of them wants to be chaste and the other part chased preferably naked through the deserted forest, it panders to their surrender fantasy.

What they really, really want

What Virgos really don't want is for you to make a fuss of them so don't go all ostentatious and big-hearted on them because they only get embarrassed and retreat into themselves. They all like to know what's going on so any information technology thing that makes their life simpler and more organised will always act as a magnet for these busy bees. The computer revolution was ready-made for these people; they have learnt new skills around functionality and efficiency that were previously undreamt of. Before computers, they revelled in digital watches or pocket calculators. They crave the information and knowledge to make their life simpler in a weird way. They like systems, clean bathrooms and people who don't smell bad as well as anything to do with body systems, health food or purification techniques.

Pisces really doesn't have a clue when it comes to saying what they want. The savvier of them are fast off the block, saying "What have you got?" They all like disguises so wigs, dark glasses and all covering clothes are always a good bet. Anything made of glass always works, with lava lamps a sure thing. They want to be surrounded by magic, by flowing and gentle surroundings where they can drift, dream and love with both imagination and passion; they want to be absorbed into the mystical and spiritual side of life seduced by the romance of the situation. For some reason they all like Arthurian myth and the archetypes that go with it. A day at the sauna is absolute heaven to Pisces, they can just sweat and melt in perfect safety knowing that at the end of the day they come back out into the real world again but cleansed and purified.

What to watch out for

With the Piscean tendency to dissolve all that it comes into touch with there is a need to maintain your boundaries against the more nebulous side of their nature. They will think nothing of taking you with them on their flights of fancy but then who pays the bill? Without meaning to be they are the best seduction experts in the zodiac. If they knew what they were doing they would be really scary. They are really good at casting an enchantment spell around their activities so that they appear to be acting always with the best of intentions but there is a sneaky side to their nature which can insinuate itself into any nook or cranny and introduce an element of doubt or uncertainty into almost any situation. They are not as wide-eyed and innocent as they seem so don't go falling for all of their victim/martyr games, because self-pity and potentials for depression are their biggest downfalls.

With Virgo, their often-quoted tendency for criticism and perfectionism can sometimes be well deserved. It's not that you don't welcome their attempts to bring a better degree of quality and efficiency into your life with their helpful suggestions but could they at least let you get your first coffee down your neck. Their ability to pick you to pieces can be their most annoying trait but the second you turn it on them they become instantly defensive, often accusing you of cruelty and reminding you that they are always doing their best and how could you be so heartless as to pick on them when all they are trying to do is improve your life? They can be defensively sneaky and picky and somehow it's always you that ends up clearing the drains or doing anything that involves smells and dirt. Like Pisces they are good at casting blame so don't buy into their purity trip too much because some of them can be real closet fascists.

How to wind them up

To wind up a Virgo is quite simple. Stand next to them on a hot, sunny and sweaty day and waft the smell of your underarm perspiration towards them, it turns them right off. Personal smell is so important for these hygiene freaks that they don't care what you look like; it's your body odour and attitude to health and hygiene that dictates their attraction. Re-arrange their bathroom for them when they are not there, moving everything two inches to the right. Moan and complain more than they do because that's guaranteed to irritate them. Leave the cap off of the sauce bottle or the toothpaste and watch them explode.

It's almost embarrassingly easy to wind up a Pisces. Accuse them of feeling sorry for themselves, that they are constantly wallowing in self-pity and that they are obsessed with finding the perfect ideal. Remind them that the perfect partner is alive but ninety-eight-years old, blind and living in the Amazon rain forest or two-years-old and living in the Himalayas. Tell them that they are being rationed to five minutes a day in the shower. Meet them at five in the afternoon on a Friday at a major city train station because the compression of people's vibes really scrambles their brains. Hide their slippers and tell them that their dog is really their familiar.

8

Venus

The exotic and sensual

The symbol for Venus is the circle of Soul on top of the cross of Matter, signifying the rise into the higher soul through transcending the need for matter, this process being facilitated by the core Venusian principle of love in its purest form.

Venus is what you appreciate and enjoy, simple as that. The quality of the material and substance that you enjoy is dictated by the sign, house and aspects of Venus in your chart but the Venusian principle is that of value, sociability, cooperation, worth and the feeling of pleasure and appreciation of beauty. The higher evolved Venus types know that real beauty is measured in quantity as opposed to quality and will go out of their way and bide their time to ensure that quality.

Venus is what turns you on, whether that's physical, sexual, financial, culinary, romantic and emotional. It's what makes you feel good, inside and with yourself at all levels. Venus is what pushes your pleasure buttons, whether that be art, food, money, sex, power, passion. It is the raw material of love, the receptive and passive, the feminine and the delicate that nevertheless knows exactly what she wants and somehow manages to convince the rest of the world that she is fully deserving of it and that they should give it to her.

Venus is especially associated with two signs. In the sign of Taurus, through its physical and sensual side, Venus learns to express itself in a manifest way. Taurus brings desire for effort in order to procure the basic values and materials of life and Venus provides the desire for these things, although not necessarily the physical energy for that procurement. In the sign of Libra, through its more appreciative and social side, Venus learns how to share both with other and others, although there can be difficulty knowing where boundaries lie and thus depleting yourself. Venus makes us want to better ourselves, to appear more pleasing and to bring both pleasure and decorum into your life, your home and family, the workplace and the relationship. Above all else perhaps Venus brings us into touch with that yearning for harmony that lies deep within all of us.

Venus is love in all of its feminine manifestations and the ways that it works at the individual level is dictated initially by the sign of the zodiac that Venus inhabits. The following guide should give a somewhat facetious guide to the qualities of Venus through the signs and the houses, remembering that Venus according to its sign position shows what it is that these people enjoy whilst Venus through the houses shows how they attract things and people towards them from the outside world.

Venus in Aries

Venus actually isn't that comfortable in Aries primarily because this is the territory of its equal and opposite planetary energy, Mars, and as a result Venus can feel quite vulnerable here. Its normal subtlety can go out of the window every so often, it has an impulsive approach to love, sex and sensuality and it can be in love with the ideal of being in love, looking for the dream and trying to create it in the moment. Consequently it acts like a man and works on the principle that the best line of defence is attack and often goes out of its way to retain the initiative.

People with Venus in Aries enjoy the thrill and spill of the chase and even the women are quite aggressive in their pursuit of what they want. Once they have vanquished or conquered you the fun of the chase is gone although at the end of the day the quarry is normally cornered in the bedroom and then the fun and the bloodletting begins. Venus in Aries is assertive and projective and even sometimes aggressive but always direct in stating what they want. They secretly love being challenged by their partner and occasionally even being defeated. They dare you sometimes to stand up to them because the thrill of the chase is amplified by a little resistance and it brings out the primal in them.

Venus in Aries loves being worshipped and adored but sometimes can play the infantile child in relationship games, often appearing on the surface as being unconsciously inconsiderate of their partner's feelings. When they start coming out with comparisons about you to their ex partners start playing the same game back or else pack your bags. Once they realise that they are in danger of no longer being your number one they will very quickly grow up and mature although the childlike behaviour will always sometimes surface. At the end of the day they are after conquest, occasionally by you of them but normally the other way round. Self-reliant, Venus in Aries prefers not to be alone but also likes to be in control, addicted to the chase and the immediacy of love and sex and at the baser level this can result in mistaking sexual attraction for love thus creating a lot of short-term potentials which only rarely evolve. Their attractions are often towards the colours black or deep red, along with scarlet and purple: they like to think of themselves and be admired by others as snappy dressers who epitomise contemporary cutting-edge culture and they are drawn to this aspect in others.

Venus in the first house

This position certainly has an effect, at times coming across like a drama queen on heat, whizzing in and taking over the joint and then whizzing out again before anyone's had a chance to draw breath. Assertive and projective of their own qualities, these sometimes over friendly but highly charming and magnetic people feel that the world revolves around them and if the outside world is too dumb to recognise that then they will move on until they find an environment that does recognise their magic and allure. They know that they are quite attractive and most of the time they come across as hot but they can turn to ice in a moment if insulted so give them no cause to be offended, especially in public.

Venus in the first house comes across in a dramatic and dynamic way and normally ends up getting what they want one way or another, especially in the bedroom. They have a real skill at getting the world to be the way that they want it to be and for making the world think that they wanted it that way in the first place. This is the position of the charmer par excellence but watch out for when the charm starts getting too thick because this normally means that there is some specific action imminent.

Venus in Taurus

Venus is at home in Taurus and at its most sensual and feelingful, it is perhaps the best place in the heavens for Venus to feel comfortable in. Venus here enjoys sensation and stimulation to the highest of both quantity and quality, although given the choice it will always prefer the latter. These physical people all love the touchy-feely side of sex and eroticism, they are into bodies big time and it doesn't really matter what the other person looks like as long as they are tactile. Sometimes people get bored with repetition but as far as 'if it's working don't fix it' goes Venus in Taurus wrote the manual and most of the updates as well. If they can't have a roll in the fields, long grass, hay or the barn then a roll in the bedroom will do as long as there is extra massage and oils. They like to feel safe and stable in their settings, making them more seductive and seducible in the comfort of their own homes although they do have a habit of suddenly stopping mid flow during sex to go off for a light snack, so play safe and keep some munchies in the bedside drawer.

Taurus is a powerful Earth sign and Venus here will sometimes really like to get down in the mud and get really dirty, in all meanings of the word but they do so with such a playful innocence that no one really senses their horniness until they have got you where they want you. Only then do you realise that you are their food. The really kinky ones like to eat their meals off of you.

They all like to feel raunchy, although given safety they settle for routine. They are certainly generous to their friends and loved ones, although extravagance can be a guilty pleasure too far. Venus in Taurus can be possessive and they don't like relationships that move too fast, preferring instead to have steady and stable hands-on experiences that aren't too frenetic but that bring consistency and stability into the relationship. It sounds boring but domesticity is their greatest trait. They invented naked washing up. Venus in Taurus abhors betrayal and will stay frosty till the end of time if aggrieved or undervalued but at the end of the day they are physical lovers who appreciate sensuality, sexuality and the frequent and experimental use of food in the bedroom. They are not given to tacky or brief encounters and consider abundance their natural goal in life, although as they get older they realise that it's not how much you or they have got, it is what they do with it that counts.

Venus in the second house

Here in its natural home Venus can grow to be splendidly generous, big hearted, magnanimous and nurturing in a way that fulfils and rewards her. Venus here has an organic and natural understanding of how to make people feel wanted whether it is in the bedroom or elsewhere. When they tilt their head to one side and start looking you up and down as though they are evaluating you then relax, they probably are. This means that you have passed the test, at least so far. The ideas of providing and being provided for brings a sense of fulfilment and the ability to manifest your needs is always going to be there. They can always lay their hands on what is needed at any given moment and if that is you then so much the better.

Be warned because they are also damn good at using resources and sometimes spending more than they have, so always encourage them to remember where their personal brake is. This also works in a gastronomic and culinary potential, because Venus in the second house often expresses its love for others by feeding them and making them feel secure and safe. Either that or they can find that as they age so the ways in which they value their relationships improve and grow with time. They come across in a sensual and caring way.

Venus in Gemini

Venus in Gemini when young goes through a decade or so of being worried about their past sexual performances until the time comes when they realise that their true 'performance ratings' aren't necessarily physical as much as mental. At the end of the day Venus in Gemini considers that the biggest sex organ is the one between the ears and to them verbal and mental intercourse is just as good if not sometimes better than any type of other. If you want to keep them hooked, vary your accent in the bedroom as well as the roles that you play and know that it's the verbal that really does it for them. Whisper in their ears during sex, describe what you are doing with them, it drives them wild.

Venus in Gemini is traditionally the world champion at kissing; it gives them something physical to do with their mouth and their tongue whilst their mind is busy experiencing elsewhere. There is the famous Geminian duality to deal with here in that these people do compare past lovers and they have been known to have more than one scene going on at the same time but this only happens in either the lower evolved types or when their minds aren't being stimulated or excited. To keep them interested, talk to them a lot and then run away.

Their wit and verbal skills are their selling point; they tease and flirt in a way that can cause a degree of suspicion. They are hard to pin down and they resist complacent relationships as they like the stimulus of an active mind and social life. Venus in Gemini is the entertainer and the charmer of the zodiac. They are light-hearted but not serious enough for many and can appear flippant, particularly in the bedchamber. Surprisingly good at commitment once they make their mind up, they nevertheless fear obligation until they stare it in the face. They know all about love because they have read every book, studied every technique and they understand all the dynamics but they have difficulty is switching the mind off and letting the body feel and know love.

Keep them variable in the bedroom to satisfy their curiosity. They flirt a lot but don't get too deep about matters of the heart. Socially as well as romantically, Venus in Gemini is naturally curious and amazed by the seriousness that others apply to their relationships. They feel as though they are the butterflies of the zodiac as far as romance goes, flitting here from one thing to another quickly. Their fickle side is their least trait, their social and communicative side their best.

Venus in the third house

Here Venus talks a good talk and indeed can talk the hind legs off of a donkey but at the end of the day talk is cheap and actions do indeed speak louder than words. If they don't put in as much physical content as they do verbal their relationships run the risk of becoming more brother/sister rather than romantic interaction. When they listen to you they watch your mouth as much as your eyes, it's as though they see your soul through your words.

They do best by adopting foreign accents in the bedroom, role playing and lots of teasing and guessing games and they consider that the biggest sex organ is the brain. For some reason they seem to prefer oral gratification as much as any other form, it keeps their mouths busy, I guess.

Venus in the third house likes to come across to the world as curious and inquisitive, often changing the immediate environment. As comfortable with sex in the mountains or the barn as much as a suite in a hotel, they prefer changing environments because it gives their brain something to do whilst the body is busy. These are the people who will woo and court you with long poems about their love for you whilst drifting on a river boat down the Nile, offering you peeled grapes whilst extolling your virtues, but you had better love them back...

Venus in Cancer

Venus in Cancer is the archetypal mother figure as far as relationships go in that they make the best organisers, the best facilitators and the best cooks! They have lots of empathy for the downtrodden, they like to feed and house the needy, regardless of their gender. In fact, most of the men with Venus in Cancer are excellent at dealing with their feminine sides. The only thing they can't deal with is ridicule or being publicly undervalued by their partners or spouses. Some of them are slightly kinky or even mildly perverted in certain areas, the real reason for which is their fear of rejection. So scared are they of being abandoned that they can resort to becoming almost subservient to guarantee affection, a path that always leads to failure. Make them feel reassured of your love for them, cook them their favourite foods and compliment them on their figures (fact: Venus in Cancer of both genders have breast fixations) before letting them have their own way over you as they fuss and care and prepare things so that your life is much easier. They like someone to make a fuss over and they all need lots of hugs and cuddles and sometimes this is more important to them than sex, although to combine them all brings the best of both worlds. They need to care and will make huge self-sacrifices in order to do so.

They make great lovers if they are not too busy pouting or being in a mood but they can be seriously grumpy at times. They are willing to compromise but do prefer archetypal role models in the bedroom. Venus in

Cancer likes its bedroom activities to be private if somewhat predictable, they need their comfort and security and if given will return it tenfold. In return for that security they will give you total attention, almost to the point of becoming servile. Don't pick on them! Peace and quiet in the home and the bedroom is their mantra, they need their emotional safety and if they don't get that safety then they can sometimes retreat into themselves to avoid pain.

Venus in Cancer really enjoys snuggling in bed, ideally with some nice food and they live in fear of rejection. The worst thing you can do to these sensitive souls is ask for separate beds. Their moodiness is their worst trait, their best is their capacity for nurturing. These emotional Venusians can be the most devoted lovers in the world just not the most inventive or creative. They persist, they are as tenacious as it gets and they are damn good at managing resources and will always manage to provide you with a good hug and a home if nothing else.

Venus in the fourth house

Here the outside world sees Venus as the eternal parent figure, keeping the home fires burning and a warm welcome with a big smile and hearty food on offer as well as lots of big hugs and if you are particularly in favour a bed for the night. Or at least that's how these people like to think of themselves as being seen. Actually they are all really a bit of a mummy's boy or girl and rarely take chances at least in the eyes of the outside world but they do have a unique talent in making people feel warm and wanted in both their lives and their home.

In private the Venus in the fourth house personality knows how to make someone feel special, they find interest in almost everything about their partner and their touch and finesse is of the highest order. Their sensuality is sublime and especially in the latter part of life this comes across as a deep affection and emotional demonstrativeness towards both their partner and all members of the family, especially grandchildren. They come across as kind, homely and nurturing with a sexy twinkle in the eye and indeed these people are perhaps the best in the zodiac at refining their sexual skills as they age, concentrating on finesse and subtlety as much as anything else. Just don't criticise their home or their family, especially in public, because you will lose a good friend if you do.

Venus in Leo

Whilst both genders are fully aware of the fact that it's hard to be modest when you know that you are the best, all Venus in Leo people remain blissfully unaware that with the possible exception of Venus in Gemini they are the best flirts in the whole world. Even the ones already in contented and working relationships keep a roving eye open, not for conquest but just to look, to see what everyone else looks like, what they are wearing, how their posture is, everything so that they can evaluate and be one jump ahead of the rest. Venus in Leo is regal, let's face it. Charming drama queens, they wouldn't be seen dead following anyone else's trend so if you want to lose them quick then tell them lots of stories about your past lovers. They like to send people off on missions and you become their best friend for at least ten minutes when you bring them things. They like to think of the rest of the human race as staff. If you are showing off to impress them then let them know that you are their inspiration otherwise they will just walk off.

Alternatively, praise them to the hilt because compliments work. Providing they are loved, adored and admired you will find the most contented and loyal lover here, just don't remind them of their lowly position if you want them to stick around.

They are all natural Gods or Goddesses, putting their partners to the test regularly to find out if they are still valued. They like a degree of inequality in the bedroom as long as it takes turns with them getting sixty per cent of the equal shares. Love and sex get intertwined too much and confusion often ensues but passion is at the top of the list. Proud of themselves, they court and love to be courted and love is the highest form of affection. A bit ostentatious, they show their tail feathers regularly in an attempt to keep you but don't get too showy yourself in their company because they will try and outdo you and then it gets competitive.

All people with Venus in Leo like to dramatize their emotions and they are all slightly offended and puzzled that they haven't yet been discovered by Hollywood. They get threatened by indifference or forms of impersonality and their need for loyalty and love is even more important than sex but only in the higher evolved types. Admire these flamboyant superstars, remind them how good they are to you and they will always make time for you in their busy schedules. They like you to be a bit jealous because it makes them feel even more wanted. They are the archetypal good time guys and gals, generous, warm hearted, proud, fun loving and always attracted to romance as much as if not more than relationship. Passion and fun are their keywords.

Venus in the fifth house

Here Venus shines like the Sun at midday; she can be at her most flamboyant and her most imperiously regal, looking down from her lofty perch and observing her subjects, occasionally picking one of them out for her personal enjoyment. Much more likely is that Venus in the fifth house will be content to take a back seat and let her creations speak for themselves. As they get older this position recognises that the best example of creativity is through procreativity and their children become their pride and the apples of their eyes. This position is famed for its romantic potential and their film star-like dreams and they are not uncomfortable with demonstrating their affection for those that they love. They want the world to see them as down to earth and grounded romantics if such a thing is possible. This is a fortunate position for Venus as it somehow has the ability to magnetize the important things in life but because of this tendency those with this position should be careful what they wish for without thinking things through properly. A warning here is that this house position of Venus has a worldwide patent on pouting so if you see their eyes shrink and their lips start pursing, perhaps it's time to reinforce your admiration for their fortitude and affection.

Venus in Virgo

Here is the archetypal Virgo personality, at least as far as sex goes. They are all quite open-minded and ambivalent about sex as long as you have had at least two showers in the last twenty-four hours, you have cleaned your teeth recently and your breath doesn't smell. Venus in Virgo views sex as a functional and necessary thing which has the added option of also being pleasurable. The typical Virgoan nitpicking and criticism can be seen as a sign of affection here, at least they care enough about you to suggest ways of cleaning up your act. Venus in Virgo all want to play doctors and nurses in the bedroom but only if things are neat and tidy in advance. You know that they are really in love with you if they don't appear to mind the state of the place, although after the heat of the passion they may well decide to tidy up.

They are either the most devout and devoted lovers or else they will dispose of you like a used wet tissue at the end of the day. Thing is though, Venus in Virgo does like to remember details of previous lovers, not for comparison but to remind them of what sex is like during their periods of abstinence. Venus in Virgo does like to do the denial thing but then when they fill up their tank they really do fill it up to the top and then they are raring to go for a long spin (just remember to pack your toothbrush).

Allegedly not the flirtatious sort, they are not interested in big gifts or promises. They take their time getting into your heart and their sensible reserve is part of their magnetism, they want to feel that they know you before they make a move on you and they genuinely tend to care for those they are with. Venus in Virgo really doesn't like show-offs or the flamboyant type, they prefer instead those who work hard enough to deserve them. Once you have found out that the way into their hearts is to value them and let them know how you will care for them, they return this love by just being there for their lovers, often adapting to the other's whims in order to feel safe. They like to help others because if it all goes their way they feel guilty. Too analytical, they need to feel as much as they think. They always want their relationships to be in a state of development, always getting better and sex is a healthy way to release tension and improve their health and well-being.

Venus in Virgo people can be a little insecure about their own physicality so make up for this by paying attention to others. They like to think of themselves as selective but strangely enough tend to be drawn towards those less fortunate than themselves. They are in danger of becoming isolated because sometimes the best sex is with yourself.

Venus in the sixth house

These can be the purists of the zodiac, insisting that true pleasure and personal enlightenment can be found only through the most holistic or devout of lifestyles but then you will find them at the back of the store, guiltily stuffing chocolate wrappers in their pockets. They are actually quite kinky in certain ways and flirt dangerously with ideas of either sexual denial or over gratification whilst at the same time trying their best to appear quite normal for the sake of acceptance. Venus in the sixth house wants to be seen by the world as being industrious with a degree of finesse, they want the world to see them as pillars of society whilst still having a little bit of risqué in their personal lives. These aren't your normal sex and food junkies as is often the case with Venus. These are the people who take vitamin pills and muesli bars into the bedroom along with lots of dried fruit. They all have a fascination for elements of health and will always strive to have clean and uncomplicated lifestyles. They are too busy worrying about their own performance to worry about others, although there comes a point where they simply shut up shop if they feel that it's too one-sided. To get into their heart, make the effort to assure them of how much they mean to you, warts and all but preferably don't mention the warts.

Venus in Libra

Traditionally the best place in the sky for Venus it certainly does bring a degree of sophistication and balance into your love life. It doesn't matter what you wear or what you look like, once Venus in Libra takes a shine to you that's it, they are hooked until you start treating them badly at which point they shut up shop, move away fast and you never see them again. They really are the epitome of teamwork in that they like to do everything together from the gardening to the kitchen to the bedroom and woe betide anyone who expects them to do more than their share in either area over too long a period of time. They like to be pampered and treated with the delicacy that they deserve and the easiest way to lose these people is to behave grossly towards them, especially in public. Problem is that both genders tend towards laziness in that they want others to do all the hard work whilst they lap up the cream. They can tend towards complacency and find it hard to take the initiative so remember to give them a gentle kick sometimes otherwise they will quite comfortably sit back and let you make not only all the decisions but also all the running whilst they just sit there and purr.

Venus in Libra will be happy with just one lettuce leaf on the plate but it has to be presented just perfectly with a degree of sophistication and elegance.

Sometimes the partner does come first but not always otherwise there will be trouble. Keep them content in your life by aspiring to be the perfect partner that they all secretly want. Make them happy by treating them as equals and you will find the most charming, sophisticated and aesthetic partner you could ask for, although they feel threatened by extreme expressions of feelings so don't go over the top with them. They truly do prefer the middle ground; going close to the edge upsets them and pushes them towards feelings of persecution. Venus in Libra likes to talk almost non-stop about the relationship and over time this will bring real success and solidity into it. They need to feel valued and wanted and in return they put themselves in your shoes and treat you the way that they think you want to be treated. They are the most diplomatic and sensitive but also cool and detached in their demeanour, great socialites but turned off by loutish or uncouth behaviour.

Watch out for their dependency tendencies because the shadow side of this can be inconsistency. They do tend to shy away from troublesome situations, preferring their partners to sort things out. Libra Venus people bring balance, leaving others to do the extremes. They simply can't stand a discordant energy or unbalanced atmosphere being around them. Subtle in and out of bed, they appreciate art at all times and in all places but won't put up with discord for more than a few hours before getting upset themselves.

Venus in the seventh house

These are the people who make the best high court judges, football referees, arbitration experts and personal counsellors, because their ability to deal with people at the one-to-one level and bring them more into the centre ground is the best that there is. They try to impress the world with their ability to see all sides and as a result will dress and behave in ways that are acceptable to all, hence their middle of the road appearance. Venus in the seventh house lives for their relationships and presents a sad sight when alone so they do go out of their way to have a loving and friendly nature and are often quite happy if their partner is the more successful one in the relationship, at least as far as the outside world is concerned. If their partner is not as much a friend as a lover then they are in the wrong relationship.

Seventh house Venus people want the world to see how good they are at interpersonal relationships and often their partner is seen as an extension of the self. If there is any type of problem with this position it is that they potentially put too much onus on the partner, expecting too much of them and thus casting themselves as subsidiary to the relationship. Nevertheless, as far as romance, relationship and all the gooey bits that accompany them go, this is the best position in the sky for Venus.

Venus in Scorpio

There are two very different sides to Scorpio as far as Venus goes. Venus in Scorpio is the best at being detached, impersonal and seemingly uncaring especially if you don't tell them the absolute truth. If you do tell them the real truth, they may still resent it but at least they will respect you for your honesty and talk to you again, although it may take time. Alternatively, Scorpio Venus will be the greatest lover you will ever have but if you are fortunate enough to get these paranoid people to open up to you don't ever betray them because once they close down it's for life. They do like excess, of all types. They will love you as much for your virginity as they might for your perverted past and what they are good at is keeping secrets, although to the more depraved or lower evolved Scorpio Venus personality this means just not telling their other lovers about you.

At the end of the day, Venus in Scorpio is concerned about the extent of loyalty and control. They will almost push you into the arms of other lovers just to see if you do. If you go there you are finished and if you don't then you pass the test until next time. Not the easiest position for Venus, the lessons of self-discipline and self-control are never far away from the front of the mind.

They can be quite complex if they let their desires get the better of them. Needs, wants and desires are the hardest thing to keep clear in terms of distinction. Sexy and magnetic, they enjoy a full range of fantasies but they don't kiss and tell, although they do compare. The appeal is not so much the promise of intimacy as more the unwavering loyalty available. Venus in Scorpio is unnervingly private (not secretive but private) and they feel safer if their partner is somewhat docile or at least not competitive. They like to explore their partner's nooks and crannies but are reticent on sharing their own until truly trusted. Unwilling to admit jealousy they nevertheless have a searing stare that can burn through solid steel.

The sensible people with a Scorpio Venus don't exhibit outward signs of control; they keep it in the bedroom. They like their deep silences. These are not the flirtatious type and they generally like to mate for life, so they take their time finding the right partner. They don't like to surrender any or part of their power, because it's all or nothing with Venus in Scorpio. They thrive on intensity, whether ice or fire. They like the more surreal, gothic and deep and superficial trends mean nothing to them. They are excellent at finding out things about you even if you don't want them to and they all unconsciously think of themselves as a modern equivalent of James Bond.

Venus in the eighth house

Venus here has to deal with a rather dodgy reputation that is ill deserved. Only a few of these people will sink to the depravity mentioned by most astrological text books, the majority of them becoming more and more aware of the difference between their needs, wants and desires and what their priorities are especially as they age. True, they do have an attraction towards the more physical side of life and this can sometimes take precedence over anything else but this physicality can be food, money or possessions as much as sexuality or sensuality. There can be a lazy side to their nature preferring others to do the dirty work and self-discipline is not their strongest trait. These are the people who can transcend lower, baser emotion and aspire to the heights of true feeling and sensitivity through a number of different avenues. Sex and Tantra are one way but so are Yoga, meditation and willing self-discipline.

Venus in the eighth house people want the world to look underneath and see them as more than they present themselves as being and once they raise themselves out of redundant fears of guilt and phobia and face both themselves and the world as being who they are, warts and all, they find a whole community waiting, acceptant of them as they are.

Venus in Sagittarius

This is the stuff of truly blue-eyed romance, fantasy movies and the potential for all of your dreams to be met if only they would stay still long enough in one place to let the dust settle. They appeal to the hippy in us all with their wide-eyed charm, naive innocence and somewhat idealistic philosophies on the value of love and relationship. Venus in Sagittarius is the type of person who will stop in the middle of sex to tell you a joke, not realising in their innocence that they have completely shifted the energetic flow. They can play the game of naivety and wide-eyed innocence to a degree that they can get away with almost anything because you are always going to assume that Venus in Sagittarius doesn't really mean it the way it came out, it's just their lack of tact – isn't it? That wide-eyed innocent look lets them get away with almost anything, it's the 'who, me?' approach to life that keeps others guessing about them. A sure way of keeping them happy is to whisk them off every so often to some far-flung land just for a change of scenery, it keeps them devoted and loyal. Most of them ascribe to the code of gallantry and many of them have strong ethics, as well as children named Merlin or Guinevere. They are the true epitome of the romantic adventurer.

These people treat sex as though it's a team sport in that they like the competitiveness of the bedroom but their patience is limited, they don't like the chase and prefer action rather than words. They like constant exposure to new things and think little of running naked through the woods or the fields being chased by their lover. They have great humour, are mildly flirtatious and have open minds but are threatened by others hemming them in and run away from emotionally intense commitment. Venus in Sagittarius people tend to go for the more unrefined types, the hidden jewel and they normally don't have time for the superficially sophisticated. Look past their innocence or clumsiness and you will find a heart of gold based on a direct sense of humour and straightforward approaches to sex and love. Complications are a real turn off, they like things to be yes or no all the way down the line.

Venus in Sagittarius knows that they are best off travelling with prospective partners because if they can live with them on the road then they can live with them everywhere. They like freedom even within a committed partnership and prize autonomy above most else so consequently neither gender is the best of homemakers, preferring to work on the philosophy that their home is where they rest their head.

Venus in the ninth house

These are the people who thrive on outdoor adventure, who want to jump on you naked in a cornfield on a hot summer's day and then once the deed is done engage you on a question and answer session, not about the sex itself but about how you feel and think about it. The world's gatherers of information and opinion, they act as a store of knowledge and are surprised by others opinions of them as being impersonal. Venus in the ninth house loves the idea of being courted and wooed in far flung and foreign lands, it's where they learn most through direct experience. They can bring this experience to play in their outside world life as well as through promoting or building bridges between different cultures, genders or philosophies. Their ability to deal with all different kinds of truth gives them an almost shamanistic attitude to life and its contents with knowledge of the world, other and themselves being the Holy Grail. Sex as a way of developing this expansion of knowledge is just simply the single best way for these somewhat innocent yet wise souls to enjoy themselves. They want the world to see them as wise, although for many they do need not just the knowledge and the experience but also the age to go with it before this occurs, which is why as the years roll by they become steadily better and better lovers.

Venus in Capricorn

As befits any personal or emotional planet in Capricorn, Venus here considers relationship and romance to be a structured and functional thing with the partner being the type of person with whom one can establish a dynasty, take them to meet your parents for Sunday lunch and consider sex something frightfully naughty and a source of guilty fun. Either that or they go completely the other way and end up having rumpy pumpy in the garden shed with someone of a completely different class.

Venus in Capricorn is very different in public as opposed to private, there is a place for everything but only the right place and at the right time. It is not a game with these people in that they really are the gentleman/the lady in the public domain and in professional circumstances they wouldn't melt ice. In the bedroom they really are the slut regardless of gender and it's often no holds barred. They all like tight clothes, the women with corsets and the men garters because this makes them feel as though their boundaries are established, plus it takes time and effort to undo them and only perseverant people make it to the end to find the pot of gold lying deep underneath those hard exteriors. Warning. Don't ever grab them in public. Not ever.

Simplicity works with Venus in Capricorn in that they like sex straight and simple most of the time, although discretion is the most valued of attributes. They like consistency and variety is not as important for them as it is for some. Because of this they like to think of themselves as controlled and responsible although perhaps they need a bit of random in order to spark them up. Their cool and detached behaviour leads to charges of normality and lack of spontaneity but they are some of the most stable people in the zodiac, attracted to goal orientated others.

Venus in Capricorn likes a structured approach to relationships based on practicality and realism. They like to be proud of their partners and are attracted to people who are good with values, money and responsibility. Career marriages can happen, often with the partners working together. Their fear of instability and rejection can drive them into premature relationships; these people are born old and get younger as they get older as far as relationships go, often only finding happiness when they are past forty years old. Frugal with money and love at times, they prefer class and distinction as opposed to the norm. The tradition and structure of family is something that Capricorn Venus is really attracted to and words like loyalty and trustworthiness are always going to be important to them.

Venus in the tenth house

To be successful in a sharp and sophisticated way, to bring a degree of effectiveness and efficiency into all of your professional, business and financial dealings and to know that whilst perhaps not everyone actually likes you for what you are, at least most if not all of them have a respect for you. These are some of the desired outcomes for Venus in the tenth house. There is the ability to handle responsibility in an almost clinical manner and whilst the ice maiden/master approach works at work don't forget to take off the mask when you get home otherwise loved ones just become staff. The friendly and sociable approach that they portray into the world needs to be the reality once through the front door because it is really at home that this position learns the fundamental rules concerning respect, structure and discipline. They want the world to see them as successful in whatever form success takes but being that externally successful is only really a ploy, an enticement or enchantment designed to lure similarly adept and sophisticated people into their web from where they can pick the best quality for their mate. Truth is, outer world success is just the magnet for relationship potential and they are only really fulfilled when their relationships work better than their careers. Sounds impossible but if anyone can do it this Venus position can.

Venus in Aquarius

Perhaps the most unpredictable position in the heavens for Venus, it is found in the most extreme cases of obsession and perversion as much as it is in the horoscopes of nuns and monks, unable to identify with the physical and intimate side of their humanity. True, Venus in Aquarius does epitomise Aquarian principles and true they can be quite robotic at times without meaning to and true, their seemingly all-powerful ambivalence to romance and relationship can be quite off-putting. Get inside that external detachment and you will find the hottest and sexiest position of the entire zodiac. It's almost as if they feel the need to outperform their partner as some type of compensation for their self-perceived emotional separateness. They are really good souls who wouldn't hurt a fly but they just don't seem to have the same hardwiring as the rest of people as far as romance and relationship patterns go. Anything or anyone that's different, fine but boredom and mundanity need not apply. It is their originality that makes them stand out as well as their refusal to become too possessive of people or things. It sounds crazy but Venus in Aquarius is attracted to anything (including you!) with an on/off switch and if it runs on batteries then so much the better.

Their take it or leave it attitude can be maddening to their partners at first but once you know them you realise that this is only superficial. They like long distance relationships, often being most turned on when you are not and often by the strangest of notions and ideas. The mind is so unusual that the idea of sex is sometimes better than the act itself and whilst they like to think of themselves as independent others may sometimes just see them as downright wacky.

Venus in Aquarius doesn't follow conventional rules instead preferring their own and they expect others to let them have their own way rather than constrain them. They like their lovers to be friends as well because they know that then they can express themselves without criticism or fear. Venus in Aquarius is more likely to be attracted to unconventional types who have their own attitudes towards independence and freedom within the relationship. They all live twenty years in the future and in the bedroom are easy going although they don't always seem to be fully there. They are all interested in the future and the quirkier you are towards them the more they will show interest in you. At the end of the day their real family is their community as much as it is flesh and blood and this includes you as long as you stay friends as much as if not more so than lovers.

Venus in the eleventh house

Here Venus demonstrates its love by caring for, working with and being in community. Their friends are almost as close as family and their position in community endears them to lots of people. Acquaintances abound but real friends can sometimes take a long time to steadily come through so these people are recommended to be selective of the levels of company that they keep if they have this position. A bit of the social butterfly there is a wandering mind into all areas of community and friend. They want the world to see them as good friendship material, loyal and reliable. They normally are and the word congenial was written with these folks in mind. Sometimes there is the impression that all this good-natured bonhomie is actually just a front or a compensation for a lack of true grounded down to earth horniness. These are the people who need to take a mud bath with their significant other every so often, to get in touch with their depraved and dirty side and let it come out under carefully managed conditions. Every so often they need to ask themselves about what they are actually doing for their friends and community and then ask themselves again 'What do I get?' They need to run away to nature semi regularly and to remember that they live in a physical body that has needs.

Venus in Pisces

This is one of the more superficially difficult positions for Venus as the Pisces mentality is that of wanting to believe the good in everyone, which as a result ends up putting people on pedestals and only seeing their good sides. This ends up in them being conned or deceived in ways that seriously undermines their long-term confidence. They can be quite aimless in the bedroom, willing to try anything once and quite happy to play the role of victim or subservience as it makes them feel wanted in a slightly perverse kind of way, although the sensible ones keep this behaviour pattern confined solely to the bedchamber. Yet despite all these potentials for quicksand and fog, Venus in Pisces is actually one of the best positions in the sky. It's the empathy, the kind and the sensual in terms of recognising exactly when and where space is needed and when to put their arms around you. Compassion and kindness are their middle names and as they age they become steadily more invulnerable to other people's attempts to influence them. They are loyal to a degree but they will leave if they see you on a one-way trip, because they know it so well in themselves that they can't bear to see it in their loved ones. The best relationships are those that have no room for guilt or pity.

Perhaps the most subtle on the surface, they like to explore all openings and are gentle enough in bed but dislike being categorized or put in a box so will go out of their way to keep you guessing. Shy and yielding on the surface Venus in Pisces can be quite manipulative underneath, insisting that you fulfil their fantasies at least in the bedroom. Their inconsistency can lead both them and you astray but they can't change this because otherwise their flexibility goes out the window. They need to beware of hang dog stories; there are only so many people who can be saved before their batteries get drained. Many commit to partners who 'need' them, making it difficult for them to be clear with themselves about what they want for themselves. Truth is they probably don't know in themselves what they really want but they will try anything once. They are great lovers in terms of unconditionally accepting anyone for what they really are although they don't see things so much in terms of black and white as much as multi-faceted approaches to individual needs.

Hard to satisfy, Venus in Pisces likes their boundaries to be vague because then this excludes no one. They can feel put upon and need to be clear in themselves when to cut their losses. Don't push them beyond their limits even if you aren't aware where those limits are because they will suddenly drop you never to speak again. If you trust and merge with them fully, they grow to trust back in a way that defies logic and rationality, bringing instead an artistic and empathic quality to the relationship that will prove enduring and permanent.

Venus in the twelfth house

Here, Venus works best by sometimes just closing their eyes and switching the mind off, just for one or two seconds and feeling what the gut instinct and the intuition are saying. They know when something or someone isn't right and the more they trust that gut feeling the stronger it gets. It's hard for them to verbalise their feelings or moods because to constrain those sensations into mere words doesn't do them justice. Their dreams and their attraction to art forms, dance, music etc. all speaks of their higher link with the universe. This is why of all the zodiac, Venus in the twelfth house is the most comfortable with its own company.

These are the people who every so often run away and retreat from society for a day or three, recharging their batteries by doing so. This searching for that unity with the world and the universe extends into the bedroom where they surrender to the rhythms of the body and allow a natural and organic flow to occur, elevating them in consciousness if only for a short time. Yet they are strangely on planet as long as they abstain from too much booze or other forms of toxins. They are so insecure that they want the world to see them as bastions of normality when really they are the most psychic of us all.

9

Mars

The erotic and sexual

The symbol for Mars is the circle of Soul underneath the cross of Matter signifying the infusion of refinement into matter with an underpinning of soul-based feeling, this process being facilitated by the core Martian principle of power in its purest form. In relatively recent times the cross of Matter has been transformed into the arrow, giving the more modern symbol of the arrow coming out of the circle.

If Venus is what you want then Mars is how you get it. If Venus is about love, beauty and sensuality then Mars is about lust, crudity and sexuality. Mars is everything that you do with the physical body from aggression, violence and warfare through to bravery, heroism and courage. Mars in your chart shows what you are like in the bedroom, down the gym, walking the dog or digging the garden. Mars is how you initiate action, how you start things and how your physical demonstrativeness is. Mars can be aggressive and confrontational but it can also be projective and assertive, it's your confidence or lack of it, it's your libido, sex drive, vivacity and masculine urges regardless of your gender.

Mars is the ruler of Aries, hence its association with the youthful tendency for both selfishness and selflessness and its feisty, red blooded and fiery nature fits very well with the impulse and direct behaviour of Aries.

Both Mars and Aries share a common love of energetic expression and direct and even impulsive action, although Aries is the urge to look inwards and establish a sense of individual identity unique to yourself, whilst Mars is more outwardly projective, promoting that identity into and onto the outside world.

The position of Mars in your chart according to sign, house and aspect shows the way that you can manifest your more assertive side, get what you want and learn to move on from what you can't have without leaving any trace behind. Mars quite simply doesn't waste time. So here is a slightly irreverent guide to Mars in the signs and the houses remembering that planets in signs show how energy manifests through you whilst planets in houses show how energy manifests in the eyes of the outside world.

Mars in Aries

Possibly the most superficially confident placing in the entire zodiac, these people ooze strength and security as long as their actions and decisions aren't scrutinised too closely. They do have a hair trigger temper and they all seem to be upset about something or other much of the time with happiness and complacency seemingly denied them by their non-stop urgency and need to keep doing something new. Other people can be really jealous of their get up and go because after all Mars in Aries is the most proactive sign of the zodiac, so don't forget to always take some of them with you if only so you have got someone with limitless energy to do the more physically demanding things in life. In return they get an admiring audience for their constantly changing new deeds and actions. People secretly want to drag them off for private one-to-one liaisons, because they think that they can soak up some of their Martian and Arian vibrancy through some type of intimate action. What they don't realise is that these people simply don't give in. When something gets to be too hard work, Mars in Aries just moves on because after all nothing lasts forever to the impatient Mars in Aries until they realise that a bird in the hand is definitely worth two in the bush.

A step ahead, they think they know what you want in the bedroom and will try to dictate circumstances. When they find that you are keeping up with them they change their minds quickly, they change their actions even quicker and expect others to deal with them directly and as simply as possible.

"Fancy waking up in the morning hating yourself" is a classic Mars in Aries chat up line, they are quite up front and have no hidden agenda but they do have a low boredom threshold so keep changing the character you play in bed with them to maintain their interest. They have got an almost insatiable physical vitality and energy about them and their mental power is almost as strong as their physical. Don't let them overpower you in the bedroom with their zest and enthusiasm, instead helping them realise that with a little focus and self-determination they can change that impulsive bulldozer energy into something far more effective and efficient. As they age they gradually realise that in the bedroom, two and two equals five and that if they just push and take then they rapidly exhaust their partners who then don't stay around for long, whereas the more they equally share their passion with their partners the more synergetic the outcome. Mars in Aries can be a rapacious bruiser or a directed and focussed arrow of concentration and the choice between the two is down to them.

Mars in the first house

These are the people who want to get things done right now, not tomorrow, not in ten minutes but now. There will be an active and energetic lifestyle that makes them a dynamic and forceful person, giving them the energy to initiate and start lots of different things, many at the same time but with only a few getting to completion. This is the strongest position in the zodiac for being assertive and projective but also carries the risk of being overly rash, inconsiderate, or impulsive. They can tread on other people's toes without being aware of it and at least as far as the bedroom goes would do well to regularly enquire about their partners' well-being and satisfaction.

Mars in Aries exudes self-confidence and will always come across as a little brash at times but if it's someone who's going to tell you the truth and be direct that you want then this is the one for you. They can be fiercely independent and perhaps sometimes unusually direct and straightforward with a low attention threshold and the attitude of childish troublemaker when things get too constrained and/or when they get bored, so they need fairly constant stimulation in order to minimize their capacity for doing things impulsively or taking risks that rarely, if ever, work. A firecracker in the sack but they only learn to take their time as they age.

Mars in Taurus

Mars in Taurus has standards, standards that will be met or else Mars in Taurus isn't going to play. It's not exactly anal or snobbish about its expectations but it does like quality more than quantity. Mars in Taurus people will dress in warm, sensible clothing that ooze class and common sense and they give out an impression of being solid and hard workers that also has with it a slow and earthy sexiness hinting at deep passion. There is always something to be done, battles to be fought and wars to be won before they will let themselves have what they need.

Mars in Taurus likes to fight for its values because only then does it consider its conquests to be of worth and it doesn't go for the air head brigade or for other types of people who don't have a degree of groundedness about them. There is the typical Taurean warmth and generosity but there is also the capacity to not only look for trouble but also to find it and it's always the other person who ends up being cast as the unreasonable one. Mars in Taurus is turned on by sensible people who know the value of having a good hot home cooked meal before going to the bedroom for long, good, hot home cooked passion.

They are not the fastest on the block but their stamina is well known. Slow to burn but with powerful tempers when provoked, Mars in Taurus prides people on their dependability and reliability. They don't rush at almost anything but that makes them reliable over the long term and gives them a powerful and earthy sensuality that helps them persevere at relationships so much so that sometimes it's difficult to get rid of them if they have decided that you are the one for them.

Adaptability isn't their strongest facet but they do keep going at a regular and constant pace (especially in the bedroom!) and normally provide the goods at the end of the day. There is the Taurean obsession with bodies and touch and they will spend hours exploring every nook and cranny of your body and have mutual fun with you finding out what these parts can do and they are not averse to receiving the same treatment as well. They mellow with age and as long as the basics aren't threatened they will go with the flow most of the time. It's the worst Mars position for bringing out sudden flashes of jealousy so don't flirt with their friends in their presence because this does bring out the enflamed bull in the proverbial china shop and they can be slow to calm down.

Mars in the second house

There will be a degree of perseverance, determination, thoroughness and durability that others may sarcastically say is just a disguise for stubbornness but regardless of description, these are the people that get things done in a proper and permanent way although it is also true to say that they may not be the fastest on the block. This is the Mars sign that most of all does enjoy hard work, tending to focus on taking each step deliberately and carefully before moving on to the next one.

Ambitious and perhaps a little careful when it comes to money, they can be quite possessive both of things and of people but at the same time they do like a physical challenge with their physical abilities and energy making up a strong part of their sense of self-worth. Stamina is perhaps their strongest attribute. The world of the five senses is important to them on both sensual and sexual levels with a hearty appetite and strong stamina for life. In the bedroom this is amplified with an earthy and almost primal approach to sex, minimizing complications and keeping everything simple and fertile. Of all the different Mars positions this is the one that recognises their cycles and swings in a way that guarantees regularity and consistency.

Mars in Gemini

On the surface, it would seem that the Mars desire for direct experience coupled with the Geminian desire for variation and difference is a marriage made in heaven but it can get a bit superficial. People with Mars in Gemini are likely to have high standards of mental community and will often judge others on their initial responses without the other even being aware that they are being evaluated. There is always going to be a strong interest in as many different things as possible as here lies the eternal apprentice jack of all trades. Gemini Mars can be the worst gossip in the world without meaning to and variety in interactions is the spice of life. In a weird type of way there is a kind of inverse loyalty to the right type of partner here if both people are able to hold a flexible and adaptable attitude towards changes in day-to-day life. At the end of the day though there can be too many words and not enough actions and perhaps it's better to act and then talk as opposed to the alternative. Although in the bedroom Mars in Gemini can probably lay claim to the world record for other more personal uses of the mouth and the tongue, another way of keeping these fertile mentalists out of trouble.

Easily bored, it needs a fresh impetus to keep levels of output high. If their mind is fertilised as much as their body they are fine but they do need to dance regularly to quieten their mind. If they don't find ways of expressing their energy they get fired up and then their sharp wit comes out, possibly running the risk of alienating others through sarcasm. They can be quite fidgety, never knowing quite where their energy should be best used. It's a restless position that needs regular sexual expression in as many different forms as possible. They like to keep their hands busy and are adaptable at playing roles in the bedroom from baby to pirate. Great kissers and fun in bed if you don't mind their incessant verbal diarrhoea, just remember that to them words are like a kind of sexual foreplay and that when the words dry up it normally means that they are finally getting down to business. If you can find a way to comfort these mentally tortured souls, they will prove to be not only the best kissers and lovers on the block but also the most focussed and concentrated in giving you their attention. There is a catch in that you have to keep them interested so every so often shock them by whispering dirty and rude things into their ear, just to see their response.

Mars in the third house

Sometimes known as 'rent-a-mouth' this position gives the immediacy to the mind, thoughts and speech that can be sharp and cutting edge but also can be blunt, clumsy and unsubtle. This is the Mars position that will speak its mind impulsively, shooting from the lip when it comes to expressing opinions. There is the desire to know a little about everything and there is also the wish to share that knowledge with others whether they want you to or not. Generally, Mars in the third house will be very direct and clear about communications although there can be the occasional tendency to easily get worked up about what others might think are trivial matters. They are all gifted with verbal dexterity to some degree or another although they can also be seen as being provocative in their communication style. These are the best teasers of the zodiac who will take a long, long time during their striptease for you. At their best Mars in the third house people can be enthusiastic, animated and lively in the way they express themselves and this can inspire others, whilst at their worst they can sometimes come across as impulsive, headstrong and oblivious to their partners' needs.

Mars in Cancer

Traditionally this is the hardest place in the sky for Mars, it tries so hard to be sensitive and feminine but instead just ends up wanting to do lots of home decorating with sledgehammers or extensive gardening works with big machines. Mars in Cancer people are in some indiscernible way tied to their home and family life thus making it difficult for them to get a life in the outside world without in some way incorporating family issues. They find it incredibly difficult to express strong emotion or anger without also bursting into tears and they are the world's best at pulling that bashful, almost shy expression of embarrassment when they are pulled up in public about something. Slow to anger but even slower to calm down, these sensitive souls need nothing more than someone to give them a hug just before they explode because this saves themselves and the world a lot of aggression. Saunas are recommended as is anything that makes them sweat. Certainly sympathetic to the moods and feelings of others, at the same time they need to keep their personal boundaries fairly consistent and stable otherwise they get overloaded, the dam breaks and floods occur leaving them useless both to themselves and to others.

They can be both dynamic and receptive, not knowing whether to be projective or not and if so, then by how much. It can all get all too complicated for gentle Mars in Cancer, so better for them to just let themselves flow with their natural bodily urges rather than try and control them. They can use their barriers and boundaries to protect themselves against what they see as predators and their libido can easily be affected by their environment. Very protective but sometimes overly so, they need to look after themselves as much as others. Give them lots of warm and intense hugs and cuddles and every so often lick warm chocolate off of them and they will be yours for life. Indifference or uncaring towards these people brings out their worst side but show them affection and care and they will never forget your kindness. Dependable and humane, they prefer to deal with things in a way that doesn't make waves and keeps the home boundaries stable if not particularly flexible.

Similar to Venus in Cancer, Mars here is a pouting champion and will use all manner of moodiness to gain what they want almost to the point of manipulation at the emotional level. Keep it clean if you have Mars in Cancer and tell people the truth about how you feel, it brings rewards in the long run.

Mars in the fourth house

Mars the feisty and fiery one in the fourth house of home and family? These are the people who can be fiercely protective of home and family but not very sensitive in their ways of manifesting this. Their desire for safety and security in their own home makes them almost parental over their partner, a habit which needs watching out for. They regularly need to let off steam otherwise the pressure cooker explodes and half the house or the relationship goes with it. Great for home decorating, building, gardening or anything involving energy and home but in the bedroom there can be a kind of passive-aggressive approach which could lead to resentment if they are not confident enough to take a direct approach to life. Often bedroom dynamics are representative of the battlefields of life but at the same time those people who they can establish close and intimate working relationships with bring an element of synergy that friends or work colleagues don't. Actions are governed by instinct and these sensitive souls shouldn't gravitate towards situations unless their initial gut instinct is good. When they learn to channel their abundant emotional energy into something more specific at the sensual level, they become warm, confident and comfortable lovers who want nothing more than the bliss of union with their loved one.

Mars in Leo

A mixture of pomposity and magnanimousness is common here, it's almost as if they expect the whole world to revolve around them and affect surprise when it doesn't happen. Mars in Leo does have style, flair, ambition and drive and if the rest of the world is too dense to see it then that's their problem. They simply consider themselves the best that there is at everything, whether it's more money, healthier lifestyle or letting their temper out and there is no possibility of anything different. There is the sense of drama that borders on the theatrical whether it's in the workplace or the bedroom especially as far as the hairstyle and the dress sense goes and there is also an element of stage queen never far below the surface that can have a hissy fit and stomp off nose in the air only to return ten minutes later and act as if nothing happened. It's cocky (it's hard to be modest when you know that you are the best), sometimes arrogant but fiercely loyal and will die for its children. A fertile, competitive, childlike and healthy Mars that doesn't like to be beaten although it would prefer to play and lose rather than not play at all. Highly creative, they do like an audience for their deeds.

The Leo Mars personality has a big heart, considering itself the dominant one of the tribe with their family often the ones that need nurturing and protecting. Of course, this can get patronising but they do love to look after their tribe. They thrive on attention and consider themselves the best lovers in the world, which can lead to obvious problems. The more insecure ones demand the world just so that they feel secure. They can come on strong but sometimes lack tact and diplomacy to the point of being obnoxious. It does bring a powerful energy which creates a high running passion towards maintaining their long-term goals. Mars in Leo is a highly physical position with sex at the top of the list as long as there is plenty of stroking and mutual admiration. Strong to rise against humiliation, they can get self-righteous under pressure from lovers and sometimes feel the need to justify themselves. The more that they can channel their passion into focussed and directed love making the more they can find mutuality in their personal relationship patterns. Warmth, humour and grandiose actions combine here to make a lover to whom power is an aphrodisiac, who can be relied on to take action and to stand up for what they believe in as well as protecting those that depend on them.

Mars in the fifth house

There will be a competitive edge to life with others or with themselves, especially when young, that drives them towards the pursuit of desire. There is a love of pleasure and they will tend to directly and perhaps impulsively pursue romance in a way that when they are older, they will look back on with fond memory. The fifth house Mars personality can be quite speculative and they are known for taking chances especially during youth. These people are not so much childish in their relationships as much as childlike; they all seem to have a healthy side to their bedroom activities that seems to involve lots of giggling and laughter.

Eventually they grow up and start taking more responsibility for both their actions and feelings although it may be that this normally coincides with parenthood. Many people with this position transfer their hope for personal achievement onto their children, thus giving those children an unwelcome burden from an early age and this is something to be avoided. Always a physical lifestyle, they are likely to actively pursue entertainment and pleasure and tend to enjoy putting on a show, whether in public or in the bedroom, being both quite boisterous and unconcerned with making a fool of themselves.

Mars in Virgo

There is the potential for the true nature of Virgo to become apparent here as this position is perhaps the most comfortable of all at being alone (not lonely but alone). They take their time getting to know people and as a result their attachments, when they make them, are normally long lasting. People with this position like their relationships to be more than functional, they want them to be clean, healthy and active almost to a holistic degree and if they can't have what they want then they will happily go without.

Mars in Virgo does make for the purist and often this can be taken to an extreme that then turns inwards leading to decadence and fantasy of the most obscure type, so they shouldn't price themselves completely out of the market. If they insist on telling those they care for about their flaws they will suddenly find themselves feeling more than a little bit alone and then they will fret about why. They do worry about their performance at all levels, they can get into a right fuss over the slightest little thing and continually give themselves a hard time until they eventually realise that they are never, ever going to be good enough. As long as there is improvement there is hope on the grounds that ninety-eight per cent is good enough and if they had one hundred per cent they would have wings on their back.

Goal orientated they are so over detailed that they can be overburdened and fragmented as a result. It's not a pushy position but they do have standards that they expect to be met and they are very protective about their lifestyle and methodology. In the bedroom they are given to anything that involves detailed manipulation of the fingers; an idle Mars in Virgo is not good for the soul. They worry when they are not doing enough for their bedroom partner and then they worry whether what they are doing is good enough. There can be an element of humility here so remind them of how much you value their analytical ability and pride them on their do-it-yourself attitude because they are the best fixers in the zodiac. There isn't anything that they can't mend or at least try to and that includes you. The Virgo Mars person loves supporting their partners and has a healthy and effective attitude towards sex that makes it not only functional but also fun. They enjoy playing the role of slave and sometimes want nothing more than to turn you on, knowing that this brings both you and them pleasure. Just don't let them put you on a pedestal because dependency is really not recommended and they can elevate you so highly that when you inevitably come crashing down they feel personally disappointed, in themselves more than you.

Mars in the sixth house

Here, Mars' capacity for physical exertion and the Virgoan tendency to do things to a fine detail helps bring a great deal of energy into their work almost to the point of draining themselves. Ideally they either work for themselves or else in a situation where no one is telling them what to do because they don't do orders unless those orders are from someone who really knows what they are talking about and who has earned respect. The industrious and effective side of this position carries itself into the bed chamber where there is a genuine desire to please others and the willingness to work at it until that objective is achieved. Their patience levels with others working alongside them can wear thin at times, another good reason for working for themselves. These people are skilled at organizing and reorganising, listing and analysing, they always put a lot of energy into their work (this includes you!) and they can get quite touchy if others intrude on their focus and concentration. If they take you on as a project to be nurtured and developed, be sure that they will pay you total attention until you reach the standard they have dreamt in for you. Either that or they become disillusioned and move on searching for the impossible dream. They become increasingly specialised and adept as they age.

Mars in Libra

Perhaps the most difficult position in the sky for Mars, it makes for someone who has to express their sense of individuality within the framework of a team of at least two and this can sometimes cause disagreements about outcomes. It's a delicate position that can be very charming and sophisticated on the outside, able to say anything in order to get what it wants but the problem is that discrimination is sometimes not high on the list of priorities. They are certainly personable in that they look others in the eye and appear interested. Even in the best partnership there will be the need for something unique; they don't let their individuality get totally absorbed by the compromises of relationships.

There can be a tendency to see the world through the partner's or the relationship's eyes, to determine their place in the relationship by reaction instead of initiative, so they mustn't be scared to act because acting and failing is better than doing nothing at all. There is a need for physical expression, otherwise anger can manifest through words, especially with partner, so there is a need to know when the flirting and banter needs to stop. Strangely subservient in the bedroom, they will do much for approval as long as they retain a degree of choice.

They think first although at the end of the day too much procrastination can lead to stagnation. The overall goal is for peace and quiet, they will always play the charming one so that they don't arouse any opposition but this can lead to such a smarmy way of dealing with others that there is just no other option than a high velocity custard pie to wipe the smugness off of their face. So scared of confrontation are they that they can become sneaky in their words so encourage them to tell you the truth even if you don't like it. Conflict management is a speciality but they do need equality in order for things to balance out in the relationship game.

In the bedroom Mars in Libra may play the subservient role in order to get your attention but at the end of the day they give and take with equal passion and prefer gentle and delicate surroundings. If you keep them happy they will always put you first, right up there alongside themselves and they make your pleasure theirs and vice versa. They like to think of themselves as diplomatic and motivated by ideas of fairness, they can charm the clothes off of your back if you are not careful but get them going and they can turn into a veritable animal. Sometimes when they do finally get going they need reminding where the brake pedal is.

Mars in the seventh house

This position brings the spotlight sharply into all one-to-one relationships, focusing on interpersonal dynamics and the ways in which people interact with others. There will always be either a powerful or an absent libido as there are no half measures here, suggesting that they will either be smitten by you or else a completely cold fish. Mars in the seventh house brings a kind of superficial ambivalence to the relationship game that only becomes more serious when words like commitment come onto the agenda. There is a need for relationships that both challenge and stimulate them and that involve being with people who can hold their own in an argument because this turns them on in lots of different ways.

Personal relationships can be a source of conflict in life if they find themselves with partners who bring out the aggressive side of their nature although this rarely comes out except when under persecution. The more they grow to understand the need for diplomacy and gentility in the bedroom, the more sign there is of maturity. There is the need to cultivate the art of compromise and avoid any potential tendency to jump down other people's throats without first making an effort to understand their point of view if they wish to maintain a degree of consistency in their close and personal relationships.

Mars in Scorpio

Sometimes this can be the ice master or maiden, unyielding and ungiving, whilst at other times this can be raw sex on a stick. One thing that it's not is middle of the road; passion is power to these sometime obsessive psychologically orientated sex magnets that have Mars in Scorpio. Long periods of abstinence followed by lots of drinking at the well, these are the camels of the sexual desert who almost thrive on the challenge of living in the barren wilderness. By doing so they know that something powerful can happen that will more than make up for their lack of the middle path.

Make no mistake, there is true passion here once melted. Sometimes the melt can take years whilst at other times it can happen almost overnight. That's why these people are amongst the best lovers, friends and confidantes as long as you treat them openly and honestly. Betrayal here will be rewarded by a life sentence of cold stares and non-communication so deal with these passionate and powerful people truthfully and you have a friend for life. There is something about Mars in Scorpio that makes one or two lesser developed types accuse them of having a black pointed hat regardless of gender but this is a reflection of their own narrow-mindedness and their fear of dealing with what Mars in Scorpio openly embraces, the opening up to and working through fear with power and love.

They love the challenge of the impossible because they need problems to maintain their edge. They are not that good at letting people in until they trust them over a long period of time but when they do trust then it is total and they will do anything for their partners. Passion slaves, Mars in Scorpio considers sex the gateway to a higher dimension and on that road they won't compromise with mundanity. It's perceptive, sharp and determined to have its own way most of the time. They constantly test themselves and their partners by pushing boundaries in order to grow stronger, although others may see this behaviour as power obsessiveness leading to opposition with others feeling manipulated or otherwise resentful.

Mars in Scorpio can surf the edges, bringing a sharp quality of both edge and depth into sex and breaking taboos if necessary or more commonly running away because of fear of their own power. Their personal magnetism is strong, making them a catalyst for attracting and activating others' energy, although used negatively this manifests purely as base lust and the descent into pure sensation with obvious short-term burn out and long-term decadence the end result. One of the hardest and most powerful positions for Mars, they need to deal with their own fears before really emerging into the adult world.

Mars in the eighth house

Still waters run deep with this position perhaps more so here than with any other position in the zodiac. Any sexual issues of anger or control need to be managed in a transparent and honest way because if not done so then there is the strong potential to attract negative energy, the like of which can be hard to shake off. As they get both older and more experienced so they become less possessive of things, money and people but also less trusting born of sometimes bitter experience. Many people with this position go through traumatic experiences in relationship patterns when young but this is primarily so that they can find out what it is that they don't want from others as they age and mature.

By a process of elimination these somewhat sensitive souls normally end up with the desired partner, although sometimes this can take decades to work out. The lesson here is that the more that Mars in the eighth house shares their fortune with others the more this is returned to them, or what goes round comes round. They just need to stay aware of how their potentially broody sexual energy can drag them into a lonely world of alienation, suggesting that they are best off keeping their contacts with other people regular and healthy.

Mars in Sagittarius

There are so many wonderful and commendable things to say about this position that it would be easy to brush the undercurrents of Mars in Sagittarius to one side. Certainly this is a bouncy and vibrant position that inspires people to go the extra mile and they have the ability to make people laugh both at themselves and the world and when necessary at you. Great position for a clown both inside and outside of the bedroom, there really can be an element of slapstick to what they do that endears them to people. Their partner(s) may take them for a romantic fool but this is representative of their desire for the world to be a better place. An attraction to the plight of the underdog needs to be moderated because at times their compassion fatigue buttons can get really pushed and they may lack discernment but most of the time there is a genuine desire to expand both their life and that of those around them.

However (and there is always a however with Mars in Sagittarius), there can be a tendency to leave major mess behind them and to avoid taking responsibility for things on their manic drive to the next big location or next big journey through life. They need to slow down and smell the coffee and not only listen to but also sometimes take the advice of those who love them enough to tell them the truth, whether they like it or not. To them, commitment is a virtue.

Their fear of commitment is best managed by constant physical expression or keeping a number of projects ongoing at the same time although like their compatriots in Aries they don't always finish everything they start and sometimes this involves relationships. Sometimes their philosophies don't stand up but they carry the day through will power and bluntness, most obviously in the bedroom where once the humour is finished then the relationship is over. Always active, they can't stand boredom. Give them their freedom and they will soon return of their own free will if you don't constrain them.

Mars in Sagittarius always gets its own way in the long run and only really gets upset when people doubt their sincerity. Their innocent and somewhat roughshod approach to sex is quite basic, the best way to manage this is to just do it and talk about it later. Very hands-on in every way, totally for the moment, they consider themselves real experience vultures. Their exaggerative side will always big you up, it's almost as if they need you to look up and aspire to and if taken too far, they can quickly become disenchanted. Build them up and knock them down is the game that in time they (hopefully) eventually grow out of.

Mars in the ninth house

There is such a quest for the truth with this position that certain significant other influences can be rode over or otherwise ignored in these people's mad rush for meaning. They are always trying to second guess you looking for some deeper or hidden meaning in your words that will give them a greater insight into your nature. Their physical and sexual energetic levels are normally quite high although sometimes it seems that sex can be just another contact sport. There will be an open-minded and almost blatantly liberal approach to life and there is also the clear tendency to be both honest and sometimes downright blunt. At least you know where you stand with these people! There can be a tendency to self-righteousness and to disregard both the opinions and the advice from others in their quest for meaning and philosophical worth but despite all this most people intrinsically trust them and find both their humour and direct approach strangely attractive.

Mars in the ninth house craves honesty from their partner and they can come across as delightfully naive and almost innocent in the bedroom. The way into their heart is through making them laugh at both you and themselves; they have a sense of the ridiculous that easily stretches into the deeper climes of the bed chamber. There is a need for a partner who resonates with their wanderlust, has an up-to-date passport and is prepared to drop everything for a bit of hanky-panky when the mood takes them.

Mars in Capricorn

For some reason people with this position are fascinated with bone structure; it's as if they judge others by the shape of their skeleton or their skull shape. Traditionally this is the best place in the heavens for Mars because Capricorn's boundaries and structures provide the perfect ground for Mars to play safely in. There is always an ethic that is governed by hard work as well as the willingness to go the extra mile to get things right. The ability to bring discipline and order into their life extends into the bedroom where they can be either quite authoritarian or else the opposite, quite subservient. The Capricorn imagery is strong here, it's surprising how often this position is found in relationships with considerable age differences with older people when young and younger people when old. Regardless of how and where the Mars in Capricorn need for action, discipline and boundaries manifests, there is a clear need to play according to the basic rules that must be adhered to, otherwise self-respect goes out the window. Here we see this position's greatest attribute, that of loyalty and a willingness to work for and trust others until proven wrong. This is the personality who learns slowly but thoroughly.

Lava moves slowly, fiery and unstoppably. This is what Mars in Capricorn does best, non-stop determined movement forward burning anything and everyone out of their way. There is a need to be aware of their impact on others and to sometimes deliberately relinquish control so that others learn to trust them more. In the bedroom this works best by listening as much as talking and sharing all types of experiences, letting the body do the moving as much as the mouth or the mind. Basically this is a grounded and down to earth fertile position that carries honour and loyalty as its badge and isn't scared to show it. They don't have a problem with trusting people once they have been a permanent feature for a long time and when those boundaries have been established, they will try almost anything once (but often only once). They like experience of all types but really dig authority in some shape or form. Some have secret spanking fetishes whilst others are into gentle forms of bondage but all of them have something ever so slightly kinky about them and if they are sensible, they make an item of this so that it brings a frisson, a mild element of edge into their sex lives. This tends to balance and counter the need for conservatism and tradition in other areas of their life and gives them something to look forward to at the end of the day!

Mars in the tenth house

This position has greater potential for success than most. There will be the willingness to work hard, to both manage and deal with authority and to become a person of responsibility with a genuine desire for success in terms of outside world rewards. They know that in order to get to where they want, they have to work hard and they will do just that. These people generally rise to a position of authority quite early in life and achieve set goals early on. They need to be self-employed although another avenue is to seek work where there is a great deal of freedom.

This position of Mars suggests work that requires lots of physical energy and brings the courage to act independently. They should learn 'people' skills as well because then choices are limitless. It's only as they get older that they start to realise that the skills they have spent so long honing in the workplace can be used just as effectively if not more so in the bedroom. Although they are late starters sexually compared to many, they more than make up for it as they age and as they become increasingly solid in their strength by middle age so they are quite willing to relinquish control to their partner and become the less dominant during their sexual escapades. These are the ones who say, "You wouldn't dare" and then pretend to be horrified when you do.

Mars in Aquarius

There can be the tendency in life to live on the fringes, to have affairs or to live in communes, to be radical in some way that exemplifies the idiosyncratic and individualistic side of your nature. On the one hand it could be said that intimacy scares the daylights out of you but on the other hand there is a need to be loved so that you remember that you are a human being and not just a cog in a machine. This need to be loved comes with conditions, amongst them and high on the list a fear of commitment until you have known the person a good seven years. There can be a superficial uncaring attitude that says that you are quite content alone and that relationship is a bonus. Obviously this is a front but there is a need to let people in and see your soft side otherwise you do run the risk of becoming alienated.

The best way for Mars in Aquarius to find relationship success is simply to refine the search into some type of humanitarian background where you will meet other like-minded souls who like you are searching for a higher existence through the medium of relationship and want to carry the benefits of the working relationship into the larger community for the benefit of more than just themselves.

No one can say for sure what makes these odd bods tick, not even them and that gives them not only an edge but also a difference. They are not as flexible as they like to think themselves as being but they do get off on mental and intellectual pursuits within the context of both community and relationship. A random approach to love and life gradually eases into a pattern that means they normally get their way. This is done in a slightly wilful but creative manner that brings partners into their lives who respect their need for independence and freedom. Mars in Aquarius doesn't do intimacy the same way as everyone else, they can be obstinate beyond belief as long as they are being pressured into doing things they don't want to do.

Although in the bedroom their reputation is quite cool, Mars in Aquarius will blossom when dealing with novel or new forms of sexual congress and the idea of impersonality can be appealing. These are the people who wear masks in bed or speak in foreign accents to turn each other on. There can be an al fresco attitude towards sex with the risk of being caught a real thrill. This position of Mars brings a real sexual eccentric whose philosophy is that they will try anything once and probably more than twice.

Mars in the eleventh house

Despite the eleventh house reputation for friends and community, people with Mars in this position generally don't have that many friends. They instead prefer to spread their energies more thinly, keeping a boot in many different camps at the same time. There will be the willingness to work with others for the common good but those whom they work with and those they socialize with are likely to be two very different groups. Always trying to enlarge their circle in order to establish new friendships when young, they sometimes take on others' problems to an inordinate degree, making them everyone else's agony aunt or uncle. It's only as they enter middle age that they start appreciating the quality as opposed to the quantity of friendships in their lives and at the same time they experience similar developments in their personal life, valuing those with whom they are intimate more and more as they get older. Of all the positions this one has the greatest longevity in terms of sex drive in that they are just as horny when they are eighty as they are when twenty. They increasingly find that cooperation becomes ever more a key word in their quest for real community, both social and intimate and ultimately, safe in their power, they become excellent relationship partners.

Mars in Pisces

Mars is a feisty and fiery planet hot on independence and action whilst Pisces is a sensitive and deep bottomless water sign so every time Mars here tries to take the initiative or make things happen it gets messy and confusion and complications can commonly occur. The best way for these people to ensure that their projective energy falls into fertile arms is not to try so hard and practice and maintain an element of surrender to the relating process, knowing that in order for good quality romance and relationship to develop there has to be an element of almost magic at its inception in order for it to be right. This can be very frustrating for them when they try and make a move on someone because actually it's best to let others make the move on them. Their intuition is their strongest tool here and if the Piscean Mars' immediate gut instinct is saying something then both they and you can trust it every time, as long as they are sober. They can play the confused and misunderstood victim of circumstances (and they do!) and they have got it off to a fine art but really they should value themselves more and find someone similar to them who recognises them as the good relationship material that most of them secretly are. It's just a question of finding someone who organically recognises that fact.

They don't like making waves and prefer passive, non-demonstrative action. Feelings of anger can promote both doubt and guilt best managed by just going with the flow and allowing their artistic traits to steadily surface. They can see the whole world as a stage with themselves as casting directors but where does the movie end and reality begin?

The typical Piscean Mars has a degree of external and internal restlessness about them, quiet on the outside but in turmoil within. They put others in positions of sainthood and then become depressed when these people fail to meet those impossible standards, often withdrawing from relationship or even society because of their impossible standards and resulting disappointment. They have a subtle approach to sex and sensuality and will try almost anything twice before they decide if they like it. They prefer the sensual as opposed to the spoken and will let you go if you wish, although they may not welcome you back. Mars in Pisces is the dreamer, the spiritualist and the musician/artist but they can be overly consumed by environment or the effects of other so need to be selective of company and place in space and regularly treat themselves to a detox at all levels.

Mars in the twelfth house

This person has a tendency to work alone primarily because they pick up so much from others around them that if they spend too much time with others, they tend to lose their boundaries, making them soluble and easily influenced by ongoing opinion or events as well as other people's feelings. There is a need for personal self-confidence to be built and the courage instilled in order to disregard negativity. A lack of self-confidence can make these sensitive souls so afraid of direct action that the natural course is to do everything indirectly. These people don't need anyone else to put them down. As they mature they come to believe in themselves naturally. At the end of the day these naturally intuitive people need to believe in their own gut instinct and their own intuition rather than the collected wisdom of the outside world and that is the same in the bedroom as well. The more they behave the way they think that they are supposed to, the more disastrous their sex lives become. Mars in the twelfth house gives both the courage and the desire to experiment, to take a small step into the unknown and to take a few chances. It doesn't automatically bring the confidence to keep trying and that's where the partner comes in, hopefully picking them up occasionally, dusting them down and putting them back on course again.

10

Venus and Mars Aspects

Sensual and sexual; exotic and erotic

A conjunction is when there are at least two planets occupying the same visual space in the heavens, when the energies of the planets in question are amalgamated and blended into one concentrated force. When the two planets in question are the equal and opposite forces of Venus and Mars, sparks can and often do fly. This is the archetypal interaction between the male and the female, the feminine and the masculine, the receptive and the projective and rarely does this flow smoothly but it always brings with it an energy of attraction and charisma into the mating game.

A Venus/Mars conjunction will be heavily influenced by both the sign and the house of the zodiac that it occupies in the person's horoscope and normally the qualities of one planet will outweigh the other, although this effect varies considerably according to the nature of the individual chart, ranging from the love of Venus to the lust of Mars. If Venus is weak, then the more gluttonous, slutty and easily swayed she may come across as being. If it is Mars that is challenged, look for hedonism, lack of persistence and narcissistic or childlike tendencies. Someone with Venus and Mars together in their chart is not going to be content with the mundane, they are going to want excitement, stimulation, passion and adventure and then some more.

The combination and blending of the two gender representatives gives an enthusiasm and a taste for almost anything, you will go anywhere and try anything at least once. There is a passion for anything or anyone that excites or turns you on, a natural and organic process, something that brings with it a kind of magnetic factor which attracts like-minded people towards you and comes across to the world in general as warm and effusive, someone who has a zest for life. There is a high level of emotional warmth and projectivity in this position but also a powerful streak that takes no nonsense. You can be charming and confrontational at the same time although this can just as easily manifest as mutual cooperation and synergetic assertiveness. This combination of planets doesn't like to be alone so actively pursues company to an extent, although it can also get angry when other people fail to meet their expectations. There will be identification with the more primal side of your nature and hopefully the embracing and welcoming of it.

Venus and Mars together breathe and exude sexuality and sensuality in ways that make other people's jaws drop and the beautiful thing here is that these people are normally blissfully unaware of their effect on other people's libidos. They don't have trouble making up their mind about whether they like someone or not and the journey to the bedroom is often quite brief as they don't appear to have time to waste! Rarely sexually inhibited (unless Saturn is involved), they can often be focussed to the point of laser-like intensity in their pursuit of what they desire especially if there is a sexual element. Consequently, they normally don't have that much difficulty in attracting relationships or getting what they want. It's the keeping of those relationships that's difficult, because they easily swing to the extremes of assertiveness or receptiveness, feminine/masculine and thus have trouble holding the middle ground whilst still maintaining the passion. Thus there will always be occasional thrusts of independence and the tendency to come on too strong or conversely periods of subservience and inhibition all of which make it a little difficult for some people to take them seriously.

This position doesn't say what their sex lives are like. For that the other aspects to Venus and Mars as well as their sign and house position need to be evaluated and built in to the prognosis. It does bring a basic desire and almost lust into the equation, although this raw passion can easily be demonstrated verbally, emotionally or physically just as much as sexually. Even then there will be fertile and sexual undertones to the interchange, this combination has a creative and procreative energy about it unparalleled elsewhere in the zodiac. If not used sexually then this energy will find other outlets, in ways that blend the more Venusian artistic and sensual sides of your nature with your Martian physical and sexual side of your being. This can be through martial art, stage or particularly through dance, however you physically evoke love.

Venus sextile Mars

The key word for a sextile is that of opportunity. The sixty-degree aspect between two points links parts of the zodiac that share different element but complimentary gender. For example, linking an air sign with a fire one, or linking water and earth is mutually complimentary, bringing ease and comfort in working together and a degree of unconscious synergy into the equation, where two and two equals five. It brings both the urge and the desire for balanced and fun relationships based on intelligence and humour as much as raw sex and passion although these are also a vital part of this combination. The partner needs to be socially adept and intellectually stimulating. This combination of Venus and Mars also brings a directness and simplicity into your life and a sensitivity and awareness of others' positions.

A natural and organically pleasing energy will attract positive attention in a number of different ways. There will be a creative and naturally harmonious way of expressing yourself, whether it be through art, music or in the bedroom. Venus and Mars working well with each other brings the chance to balance your own emotional desires with the desires and needs of others, it balances your own individual strengths with the genuine desire to reach out and help others. It's neither overly passive nor assertive and in the bedroom this creates a playful and exploratory ambience that is hugely enjoyable and mutually rewarding.

There is a balanced approach to sex that acknowledges the importance of sharing, or giving as much as receiving and of pleasuring each other equally. There is also the willingness to both initiate and receive in equal measure and to experiment with a smile. You will put your all into your relationship although it also has to be said that once you turn off, you normally turn off for life. There is a natural and flowing ease with both genders in both gay and straight situations and an ease in negotiating some of the more sticky sides of human dynamics.

There is always a degree of elegance and charm as well as enthusiasm about these people, they seem to come across as sensitive and tender whilst also decisive and initiatory. Naturally popular, they seem to get on with everybody easily although they do have difficulty with the more 'sheep-like' person who doesn't actually do much apart from follow others. Half the reason for their popularity is that they are straight, they don't play games and they look you in the eye when talking to you. They carry a social congeniality where they blend into and out of most situations like the slick and smooth operators they secretly are, talking about art, music, the latest movie or anything that creates intelligent interest and cheerful public interaction. If there is a problem here it lies either in the potential for taking others for granted and suffering in silence when others don't fulfil their secret hopes or in the potential for both complacency and laziness. There is a need for fairly regular stimulus in order to maintain forward motion and this stimulus comes from the significant others in their lives, both in and out of the bedroom. This aspect alone is one of the very best that there is in terms of relationship ease and compatibility.

Venus square Mars

A square is a hard angle of ninety degrees that puts two signs in touch that have nothing in common with each other, in different element and gender and that bring a degree of challenge and difficulty into the equation. With Venus square Mars the individual will always find themselves in various states of conflict, both with themselves and with others and the ways that they manage these challenges goes a long way to dealing with basic anger issues in the chart. If Venus is the strong one in the square then the masculine and assertive sides of your nature can be sublimated into coming across as either overly receptive and passive or too effeminate, regardless of gender and being put off by the gross sides of life.

If Mars is the stronger, there can be impulsive behaviour based on jealousy or feelings of inadequacy and clumsiness. In either case there can be dissatisfaction with expression, either by yourself or by other. Men with this aspect can sometimes seem unintentionally coarse and insensitive, whilst women can occasionally seem oversensitive or emotional. Emotional and sexual tension will run high at times and this aspect does suggest emotional problems with the opposite sex when young. At the end of the day it is better to express yourself than not to, so rather than bottle it up inside and create later explosions express yourself and hold the best of intent whilst you do it. Sure, you will screw up sometimes but you get better as you practice. This is the astrological angle that the saying 'fake it until you make it' was invented for. The way to resolve most of your emotional conflicts is to walk your talk whilst at the same time doing your best to be aware of others' feelings.

Venus square Mars can be a sexual nightmare and a real passion victim at the same time. There can exist the impulse towards eroticism at its most acute and briefest. These people know how to have really great sex and a good argument simultaneously. It's not the sex of gentle, sensual and delicate loving, it's more the sex of immediacy and stimulus, bordered with the heat of impulsive anger and emotional temperament. The amoral with Venus square Mars have little problem with personal gratification and everyone with this aspect goes through times in their life where they blow hot and cold regardless of attention and stimulus.

When young, these people find difficulty getting their timing right and there is always a degree of angst or anger driven competitiveness present, although they are just as quick to forget about things and move on as they are to get angry in the first place. They are people prone to love-hate relationships with others, indeed "There is a fine line between love and hate".

Any type of authoritarian role model is not going to work, whether that is parental, work orientated or relationship based. Partners are constantly being evaluated as to whether or not they are meeting expectations, so when young the person with Venus square Mars will often go through a different range of relationship experience, primarily to find out what it is that they don't want and perhaps spend considerable time alone, putting their sexual energy into their creations at the artistic level. Their perceived awkwardness in relationships is primarily in their own head and rooted in childhood anger patterns but as they age, they learn when to take action and when to sit back and await developments. Sometimes they feel ignored when not responded to, yet at other times amazingly insensitive to their effects on others' feelings; they often project their faults onto others as a kind of mirror. Thing is, they sometimes really, really do want to be alone but in their heart of hearts they couldn't bear to be away from the cut and thrust of relationship for too long without feeling as though they were 'on the shelf'.

Venus trine Mars

A trine links two planets in signs of the same element bringing a natural and sympathetic flow of combined teamwork and high personal output into the life equation. It is an organic and inherent talent that seems as though you were born with it. You were and you get mildly bemused when complimented on your energy. Venus trine Mars brings two opposite forces into a kind of symbiosis of understanding, a partnership based on difference but similarity and occasional examples of friendly competition. It brings a degree of balance into all of your interactions with members of the opposite gender and helps you hear and be heard with equality and sharing.

Artistically energetic at all levels of life, there is also an emotional creativity both in and out of the bedroom that constantly recharges itself. You seem to know how to appeal emotionally to others and can easily relate to both genders. This aspect doesn't guarantee relationship success but it certainly helps considerably. In order to get what you want from others you have to make concession occasionally and your willingness to do this is a mark of your maturity and personal strength.

Your feelings and actions work well together most of the time and you can normally express yourself in a dynamic yet refined way. One of the good things about this aspect is that the sex life normally extends healthily well into old age, the desire that fuels the physical engines will always be able to generate itself when the situation arises. There is always going to be the passion for romance and most people will appreciate you for the way you don't beat around the bush and normally come fairly straight to the point for example, your place or mine? Peculiar to the Venus/Mars trine is the quality of affection in its purest form that you both exude and receive, regardless of gender differences. This is a classic aspect for plain and simple sex appeal, these people are quite basically sex on a stick with the proviso that it's on equal terms or not at all and once they actually stop talking about it and get into the bedroom then they are great at resolving and ironing out even the most inflexible of kinks in their partners' armour.

One of the reasons why people with Venus trine Mars get on so well with people is that they don't try to cover up errors. It is easier to be up front with people and your ability to admit your mistakes and clumsiness in a charming and direct way improves both your popularity and your reputation. If there is a danger with this aspect, it is that of complacency. If everything comes your way naturally what pushes you into trying? You may also find that you are more susceptible to flattery than you think so sometimes objective opinions from those you trust do help and should be listened to. Otherwise your easy-going nature could easily descend into infidelity or you may easily get caught up in other people's games and then you are rapidly going to become just another puppet on the string. Providing you hold a stable balance most of the time, you will find that you become almost a counsellor to many around you and that you are seen as able to bridge situations and find common ground when dealing with other people's interactions.

Venus opposite Mars

An opposition brings two different forces directly into confrontation with each other normally resulting in challenging situations that never really get totally resolved to complete satisfaction. This is one of the rarest aspects astrologically with considerably less than one per cent of the world's population having it in their charts but it brings into stark clarity the need for both independence and integration between feminine and masculine attributes. Often this is found in the charts of powerful athletes, politicians and other forms of achiever. It can be that the emotional challenges of having these two planets in opposition is so great that the route to sensual equality can be a bridge too far, resulting in sexual and sensual energy being diverted into career, sport or other forms of creative behaviour. This aspect is as common in the charts of celibates as it is in the charts of same sex relationships. It has an eroticism all of its own with elements of domination one way or another being common.

Venus opposite Mars has the greatest capacity of all for sexual expression although in reality rarely does this come out primarily through sex. Emotional swings and temperamental outbursts can be common and these need managing for balance in relationships to occur. When young there can be a tendency to select partners purely or at least primarily for their sexual compatibility, only realising when older that whilst this is an important part of the jigsaw it is not the only part. As a result of selecting primarily on sexual compatibility grounds, there can be a degree of awkwardness in other situations such as in the kitchen or on the social scene where timing just doesn't appear to gel. Depending on the nature of the individual chart either

Venus or Mars will have the strength. If Mars there can be the capacity for riding roughshod over others' feelings, concerned instead only with your own sexual gratification.

If Venus, your mood can swing from love and harmony to irritability and frustration with apparent ease. You can find yourself holding back when projection is called for, or being clumsy when subtlety and tact are what is needed. In either case when you realise that your sensual or sexual needs aren't being met you are unlikely to hang around for long. There can be a desire for constant sexual affection and attention and you are willing to give it as much as receive it but sometimes it seems as though the timing is off or that things simply don't gel. Regardless of other factors you need to be partnered with someone with complimentary Venus and Mars positions to yours in order to fully enjoy all aspects of relationships.

Diplomacy is a foreign country with this aspect, yet you can be surprisingly hurt by the unkindness of others, whether meant or otherwise. Co-operation in relationships is often one of the hardest lessons as behaving towards others equally is never easy, either being aggressive or subservient. Learning how to express your magnetic sexual energy in ways that are not challenging to others takes the refinement of the years but eventually after many trying times this aspect turns into a consummate lover caring as much for others' pleasure as for their own. With the Venus/Mars opposition you will either run towards or away from strong expressions of feeling and emotion and although quite demonstrative yourself are uncomfortable around pushy people. Be careful about finding faults in others that are just reflections of your own issues.

11

Uranus

Daring to surf with freedom

The first of the outer planets to be discovered in the mid-late seventeen hundreds, Uranus was seen for the first time and became recognised simultaneously with both the American and the French revolutions and at the same time as the birth of a number of the founders of the Industrial Revolution. From these facts alone it is obvious that Uranus is synchronous with the awareness of the concept and practice of change at the individual level.

Since the discovery of Uranus, the rights of the individual have become ever more enshrined. Uranus can be seen as a faint electric blue blur in the night skies when there is no light pollution but most of the time it is invisible. Whilst not representative of the truly un and sub conscious (see Neptune and Pluto for these domains), Uranus comes to the surface periodically, manifesting as both the need and the energy for change, either consciously and willing or kicking and screaming.

An example of how Uranus is different to any other planet can be seen by the fact that it spins on its axis at ninety degrees different to any other planet, its poles being on its equator.

Uranus in a challenging way can bring real difficulty if ignored. Its demands for self-expression and individuality will always come through, often manifesting in unexpected ways. Uranus is the chaos bringer and, in its wake, come the attributes of unpredictability, disruption, sudden action and other dramatic changes that can suddenly pull the rug from underneath your feet without a moment's notice. Uranus has an active dislike of all ruts and routines that lead to increasing convention, orthodoxy and regularity. The more your life gets into a rut, the more complacent you may become and then Uranus will strike out of the blue, leaving you suddenly and dramatically bereft. It is the randomness of disorder, the futuristic quasi anarchist and even at times the nihilist, destroying everything in order that uninhibited change can occur. It is the shocker and many people with a difficult Uranus position have a preponderance to static electric shocks, something that can be ameliorated by the carrying or wearing of a little piece of amber (I don't know why this works but it does).

Uranus is the future bringer and people with this element of chaos in their lives will always live a little dangerously. The selfish types with a difficult Uranus position may become the archetypal megalomaniac or dictator whereas the more humanistic types will strive to evolve into and benefit the larger community, whether that is local or global.

In a favourable way Uranus brings stimulus and excitement into your life although never quite in the way that you expect it to. It is the future bringer, the unconventional and the original. It is the inventor in us all, the side of our nature that is attracted by the different and the stimulating. The keywords for Uranus in a good light are along the lines of freedom, liberty and excitement as well as novelty, originality and stimulus. It is where we not so much break boundaries as bend them, where we can dare to be different knowing that by doing so we are edging the world ever so slowly into the future.

Uranus is common in the charts of inventors, innovators, revolutionaries and radicals as well as extremists of the more chaotic type. Uranus in a good light will always bring the eccentric and the unusual to the fore, it's where you can express your true individuality and identity in a way that makes you different from anyone else. Above all else Uranus brings change and without change there is only stagnation and ultimately entropy.

Uranus through the houses

Uranus is the planet of individuality and uniqueness and the house position of Uranus in your horoscope will show which area of day-to-day life and outside world interaction you express your sense of individuality in at its most manifest. The following is a guide to Uranus through the houses and should be taken in a light-hearted manner:

Uranus in the first house

One of the most idiosyncratic placings for Uranus, the first house of the relationship that you have with yourself is a natural home from home with Uranus' pull towards all that expresses freedom, liberty and self-development. Here is the suited city gentleman wearing a pink beret or the otherwise sedate till worker who secretly goes parachuting at the weekend. It has such an urgent pioneer spirit about it that the idea of taking things slowly and gently doesn't normally occur until after forty years of age. This is the archetypal position found in the charts of people who have an active zest for life. It brings an urgency bordering on clumsiness and certainly is not the best position for tact and subtlety, let alone diplomacy. It will try anything once, it is one of the true explorers of the zodiac and works on the principle that it's better to learn by direct experience even if it hurts than it is to learn by text books or teachers. Uranus in the first house has an electric and magnetic charm that is very seductive until you realise that these high-octane burners of life inadvertently use other people as fuel, quickly burning others out and moving on. It takes a lot to keep these dynamos still and quiet, action is their forte.

In the bedchamber this position has to go through a number of difficult experiences in youth in order to find a degree of balance. The way they find out what it is they want is via finding out first what it is they don't want, slowly narrowing down their options and making their choices fewer and fewer until what's left has to be pretty good. They can elicit charges of selfishness and only learn about equality and mutual satisfaction as they get older and wiser. Uranus in the first house is wide open to experimentation and they will try anything once and often twice as long as it's not painful. They can be sensation seekers and often don't settle down into long-term committed relationship patterns until their early thirties, preferring instead to sow their wild oats when young. Once they have got the hang of the fact that their partner is not just there for their use or convenience, they can turn into surprisingly sophisticated and gentle lovers because they realise that the more their partner enjoys the experience the more they will as well and they can mutually discover that sex is as much a pleasure as it is a release.

Uranus in the second house

One of the hardest positions in the sky for Uranus, the second house is known for its durability, resilience and possessiveness, all of which makes the freedom loving side of Uranus distinctly uncomfortable. There can be a fear of clutter and disorder and often someone with a difficult Uranus in the second house will forswear the materialistic side of life and become practically an ascetic, living with as little as possible. The alternative but equally extreme manifestation of this position is 'the old woman who lived in a shoe', seeking for that internal security and stability through the process of accumulation and the amassing of possessions in an effort to attain materialistic solidity.

The sensible ones with this position of Uranus generally end up with relatively little in terms of actual possessions but what they do have is normally of the highest quality. It would be very easy to substitute food into the equation with the same criteria of quality as opposed to quantity. This person will never have the value systems of their peers and they either learn to walk lightly on the earth or they get weighed down with the excess baggage of life.

When it comes to their bedroom activities, they can be surprisingly hedonistic and unconcerned with point scoring. Much of their lives are concerned with finding value in what goes on around them so the bedroom is seen as a haven for fun, light-heartedness and good old indulgence. These are the people who came up with the chat up line, "How would you like to wake up tomorrow hating yourself?" To them pleasure is very much in the here and now. Once they realise that they can't buy love, that it is a currency that can only be enjoyed, not saved or exploited, they become sensual and appreciative lovers. They will try any sexual position possible once and twice at least if it involves food. In fact the more food enters their sex lives, the happier they can become. These are the people who don't care what you look like; they are attracted to you because of your value system as much as anything else. There is always the short cut of dangling a strawberry in front of them whilst licking your lips which is guaranteed to arouse and raise their interest. The sensual hedonists of the zodiac, they embrace bedroom diversity and the more it has to do with food (organic of course) the better.

Uranus in the third house

Here Uranus is in its element, that of fast and constant movement and communication at all levels. The third house governs your immediate local environment and those people in it, as well as the ways in which you interact and communicate with that environment, so Uranus here provides a real spark and dynamism into your output. It can get opinionated almost to the point of aggression especially when its ideas are challenged and it can become fiercely defensive and possessive of its visions and expressions of the future. It's their way or no way! At the same time it gives a very fertile and elastic mind that goes into the crannies and nooks that other minds don't go to and whilst it's there Uranus makes a comprehensive list of everything it is experiencing so that it can call on the memory should the need be.

Uranus in the third house collects memories, it rapidly becomes the apprentice jack of all trades knowing a little about everything, which gives it the ability to dance and jump between concentration and focus to something completely different and back again within a split second. Scatty and eclectic and frustrated geniuses on the side.

This is a slippery position for Uranus, perhaps in the literal meaning of the word. They can wriggle their way into or out of anything or anyone, it's as though they coat themselves with oil that makes them difficult to hang on to and they do have very, very slippery tongues. They will lick every part of your body, so secret one or two surprises about yourself if you know that they are in an inquisitive mood in the bedroom and sometimes keeping their tongue busy with licking is the only way to shut them up. Less words more action is a suggested mantra for these talkative lovers who seem to have the gift of the gab and need to be sometimes reminded of the matter at hand, namely, you. They all love being teased and tickled and they are all really good at the banter that sometimes takes levels of bedroom activity into situations of real hilarity. It has been said that to these talkative lovers, the biggest sex organ is the one between the teeth. If you really want to grab their attention in the bedroom, turn their mute button on and stop them talking for an hour or so.

Uranus in the fourth house

This is where you will find the archetypal family rebel. The fourth house of home, family and tradition is a place where the convention and safety of mummy and daddy bring a nestling and desire for safety and security, completely antithetical to the revolutionary and freedom seeking side of Uranus. This is where you will find the black sheep of the family, someone who often does exactly the opposite of what is expected of them by their traditional family structure just to accentuate their independence and their concepts of freedom. This is the person whose concept of home can just as easily be a backpack as it can be bricks and mortar in that they don't normally attach too much value to property or possessions, preferring to an extent to make it up as they go along. One or both of their parents is likely to have a considerable degree of difference about them, not so much absent as eccentric. Hopefully, the experience of parents when young was that of being encouraged into expressing a sense of uniqueness as opposed to the alternative Uranian way of expression, that of totalitarian and authoritarian imposition. It can sometimes seem as though they live their lives in a constantly changing and moving vehicle that is not sure which lane it should be in.

There is definitely something weird about Uranus in the fourth house though and this comes through in the bedroom. Surprisingly restless, it's hard for them to blend their Uranian ideas of freedom with the fourth house need for cuddles. So these quirky home lovers bring diversity into the bedroom. Here you will find the toe suckers, the ear nibblers and the ones who will always try something new, especially if it involves exploring new places on your body or speaking in a foreign accent, or bringing a variety of accessories into the bedroom.

Other times they imagine themselves and you in a caveman/woman situation, the idea here being to constantly keep things between the sheets in a state of stimulus and originality, thus avoiding boredom and mundanity, which is guaranteed to turn them off for a long time if not for life. The blend of safety and freedom is never easy and sometimes this combination can be a little deviant but never overly dominant. Here are the mild bondage freaks, the diaper wearers and also those who primarily just want the security of a good old fashioned nestle and cuddle.

*

Uranus in the fifth house

Traditionally this is one of the hardest positions for Uranus. The fifth house can be so expressive in its creativity that it can sometimes acquire 'airs and graces' which Uranus will then delight in collapsing like a house of cards. There is something of the childish brat with Uranus in the fifth house, the imagery is that of the child that won't take responsibility for their actions and wants everything their own way regardless of the circumstances or the consequences. Obviously this is not conducive to mature and adult behaviour and can be seen by others in your life as childish and spoilt. It is as if you expect others to naturally recognise your right to rule the roost and when others try to slap you down the childish monster within suddenly turns into an all devouring ogre. The other side of the same coin says that instead of behaving in childish ways that alienate people, the opposite and positive childlike ways of behaviour can really endear you to those same people. Childlike as opposed to childish brings with it an energy of fun and pleasure, a kind of wonder at the creative potential of the world and the joys of new discoveries through experimentation and exploration.

With the reputation of the fifth house being closely affiliated with that of romance and love, it would be easy to expect this position to be the consummate lover. This is not the case in most examples as the self-awareness of Uranus in the Leonine orientated fifth house can create quite a degree of posturing and pomp with little underlying substance. When the individual can rise out of childish gestures of insecurity and put their partner equally alongside them on their self-created pedestal there is the capacity for a real animal of passion in the bed chamber but that animal can be slow to rise and very slow to calm down.

Finding a steady level of balance is difficult for these people who so want to be liked yet find it difficult to fully cooperate with other(s), often carrying childlike behaviour patterns into the outside world. The way out of this conundrum is to allow the child within full range in the bedroom, to laugh, tickle, giggle and generally have a fun time with partner and then to leave the child in the bedroom when you step outside back into the adult world.

Uranus in the sixth house

As with everything Uranian, there is little or no room for compromise or halfway measures with this planet of incisiveness and occasional extremism.

The sixth house with its Virgoan attitudes of effectiveness and efficiency can sometimes be a place of over-zealous and critical sharpness as far as Uranus is concerned and it can rebel against what it sees as the overly focussed and concentrated ways of expression that the sixth house likes to use. Occasionally this can manifest in a person's life as an extremely slobby, totally superficial disorder and a general untidiness, all externally representative of disorder within the individual.

Alternatively, Uranus in the sixth house when it is in good aspect will bring someone who sees themselves as sharp and on the cutting edge of contemporary culture, someone who brings novelty at the same time as focus into the equation of life and a person who will take not only responsibility for their physicality but also consciously work to improve their health, nutrition and general well-being. It can be hyper critical but more of yourself than others.

Definitely kinky at least in the privacy of their own minds, this position can be the most promiscuous of all as well as the most prim and proper, often both at the same time! They are fascinated by bodies, often viewing their own with a state of surprised detachment as though it is a uniform of some kind that they wear for conformity. They will spend many hours exploring you, licking, tickling and caressing every spot on your body until they know it as well as you do. Here are the people who like to play doctors and nurses and are quite comfortable about dealing with all types of body fluids as long as they have got a shower next door to the bedroom or in the immediate vicinity.

The sixth house has a Virgoan extreme edge to it which can become very fastidious or even anal when it comes to hygiene and body odours but at the same time harbours a guilty secretive side to their nature that really wants nothing more than to roll around naked in the mud and get downright dirty. If they are sensible these people will keep their extremes to the consensual areas of the bedroom, where they can become playful and innocent as opposed to repressed and sordid.

Uranus in the seventh house

This is a relatively difficult placement for Uranus, because the seventh house is naturally inclined towards the concept of teamwork and partnership whilst Uranus is not one for compromise or meeting others halfway. Challenging aspects to Uranus in this house can indicate difficulties in meeting the constant interaction of minds and hearts that dictate conventional one-to-one relationships. There can be a high level of personal freedom issues, sometimes accompanied by spontaneous and rapid development of boredom matched with alternative and new desire for something different. This obviously makes normal and regular relationship patterns quite problematical to sustain and maintain.

Yet these people often do find themselves in long term working relationships, it is just that they are based on autonomy, or a kind of freedom within the confines of the committed relationship that suits both partners. Often the partners will have their own separate lifestyles, career and friends. The desire for relationship and the recognition of individuality brings two otherwise independent souls into co-operation based on mutual respect and teamwork.

In the bedroom this can be a surprisingly passionate position providing a basic criteria is acknowledged, this being that there has to be a mutual and shared responsibility for keeping the relationship exciting. As soon as it becomes one-way traffic for too long there will be fretting and eventually discord. Both partners have to keep the relationship alive by actively contributing to the sexual dynamic, changing the roles that you play with each other, speaking in foreign accents, dressing up in different ways and keeping things interesting and stimulating so that all will be well. Once convention becomes the norm for too long there are problems that may quickly become insurmountable.

As with everything Uranian, boredom can be a problem so actively encourage each other to take a few chances, to live life just that slightest bit dangerously and not be too orthodox in your approach to your mutual love life. At the end of the day when two people walk out together hand in hand proud of each other, their idiosyncrasies and their very nature, then there is the basis for a good and healthy relationship based on autonomy, in the relationship because they want to be, not need to be.

Uranus in the eighth house

As befits the Scorpionic nature of the eighth house Uranus in this position often manifests in some degree of extremism. Uranus placed in hard aspect in the eighth house can bring extremes of phobia, paranoia or other form of disempowerment especially when young. The other side of the same coin is that through study of the more arcane and esoteric, the individual with this position gets an understanding of the true nature of power and how it manifests in the world and they can then become a person full of power, or powerful. This is where the real scholars of the unknown live. These are the people who look at you and it is as if their eyes suddenly shift in intensity and all of a sudden they can see right through you, they can burn through solid steel with their gaze if they are provoked. This is the land of Sherlock Holmes, constantly giving a new slant and finding new ways of seeing through old problems in a way that can be quite scary to more conventional people. If there is a problem with this placing it is that sometimes these people can be quite ruthless, upon themselves as much as if not more than others.

As far as the bedroom goes, depending on the individual's sense of morals and ethics this position can take you to heaven and take you to hell sometimes at the same time. It can be the home of forbidden fruit where the temptations of power, eroticism, control and lust truly can dominate, sometimes resulting in major inconsideration for others. Other times this position brings a willingness to experiment in ways that many others would consider either scary or outside of their comfort zone in some way. What you won't find here is the surrender victim. In the bedroom these people are willing to take their turn as long as there is trust, equality and complete discretion. They will try anything once to the point of taking risks, with the need for freedom overriding conventional boundaries at the sexual level.

They are often celibate for long periods of time because the difficulty in handling that level of sexual intensity that they can sometimes produce is too much for them and it's easier to just shut up shop. They just have real difficulty with compromise regarding their need for freedom and liberty and rather than train themselves and their partner to that level of exquisiteness where they can be truly free with each other in a committed and autonomous way, they would rather go without.

Uranus in the ninth house

If there is one house that is always seen as future looking it is the ninth and Uranus likes all things futuristic. This is where the big ideas concerning the future of humanity, the planet, space and time travel and such like come from. The ninth house is where the explorers live and Uranus is always up for something new and innovative so the blend of the two is somewhat special. Whilst the combination can be at times a little light on the practical side, the idealism and the visionary qualities of this position brings a hopeful and optimistic attitude in their approaches to life.

These are the people who will drop everything and go anywhere at a moment's notice for no other reason than that they can. The idea of doing something that they have never done before, or going somewhere they have never been is always going to win out over normal orthodox and conventional lifestyles if Uranus is strong in this house. These are the direct-action merchants, to whom actions will always speak louder than words. As they age, the sensible people with this position tend to go for a better quality as opposed to quantity of experience.

When it comes to the realms of the senses, particularly those below the navel, Uranus here is in a very healthy position. This is the person who will travel to many different cultures and study various techniques to enhance their performance and understanding of all things sensual and sexual. They will master the Kama Sutra, spend lifetimes sourcing the most powerful aphrodisiacs and cultivate all types of magical and aromatic herbs, spices and secrets in order to gain a greater understanding of the power that lies behind sex.

Thing is, it's all very well knowing this stuff but the reality of it is putting it into practice and that can sometimes be a little too basic or physical for these high-minded lovers who want to make love with you in a gondola, or in a hot air balloon but to whom the bedroom can be very enclosing. Let them run naked in the countryside every so often as this will ground them and remind them that they do live in a physical body that has needs. They are not very good at taking hints so if all else fails, metaphorically hit them over the head with your club and drag them into your cave.

Uranus in the tenth house

Uranus likes to bring with it a degree of contentiousness and even radicalism, whilst the tenth house is similar to Capricorn with its elements of tradition and solid structure, so the combination of these two influences isn't always comfortable. There can be considerable challenge in conforming to archetypal career structures and their hierarchical disciplines and there can also often be difficulties with keeping to a rigid and inflexible work timetable.

If Uranus is prominent in this house in your chart perhaps it's best to consider either working for yourself or working in a position where you are not under scrutiny or pressure. Independence in the workplace will have a strong pull and can only be ignored and constrained for so long before a gasket blows and dramatic change can suddenly occur. So rather than have an argument with the boss, why not just subtly revolutionize the way you work and learn just what you need to know for your long-term plan of self-determination. It's not exactly subversive but Uranus here can get quite corkscrew-like when faced with professional dilemmas and will go out of its way to avoid routine and normality. These are the people who come up with unusual solutions to old problems in ways that make others around them scratch their heads.

Those with Uranus in the tenth house should exercise a degree of caution in the more extreme areas of the bedroom as there can be problems recognising boundaries and limits, whether your own or those of others. There is a kind of antipathy here as the structures and disciplines of the tenth house don't fit that well with the Uranian desire to break boundaries and rules. At times issues of control may enter the foreplay and as long as that is consensual and private there is nothing to worry about. There can be a real risk factor here in that the chance of being discovered doing something daring can be a real thrill.

At the same time there can be a pleasure in being controlled or doing the controlling, again within acceptable and mutual boundaries. These are the people who will wear Lycra to bed, the combination of being held in tight yet electrical and slippery at the same time being very appealing to these introverted and slightly kinky hedonists. If you have this position, remember to take turns in whatever you do behind closed doors and all will be well. It's only when things get imbalanced that problems arise.

Uranus in the eleventh house

Perhaps the most comfortable position of the zodiac for Uranus in terms of house placement it gives a natural magnetism towards groups of like-minded people and a general attraction to the type of community that is essentially futuristic and outside of the ordinary. If you have this position then one of the things that links all of your friends is that none of them are normal. They are all different in some way or another and it is that difference that makes them interesting and that they are attracted to you as much as you are to them. There can be impatience with what you see as the slowness of the world and often this position is accompanied by a kind of rugged exterior that hides the more flexible and willing side of your nature that only really comes out when you are with others of a similar ilk to you. There may be difficulty when young in learning the lessons of perseverance and determination on the grounds that as soon as something gets boring there are always new horizons just around the corner. Uranus in the eleventh house is always in danger of living so much in the future that it can easily neglect the present.

This is the position for the experimental, the futuristic and the group orientated approach to the sensual and sexual sides of life. With Uranus in this position you are not going to be too concerned about committing yourself to one person at too young an age because you will be dimly aware of the huge range of possibilities that await you in the future. Your attitude towards your lovers isn't going to be determined by what they look like, their religion, colour, age or even gender. When young you will be attracted by other people's desire for freedom and independence within the confines of the relationship and when older it is a condition of relationship that your lover must first of all be a friend.

The sensible ones with this position enjoy role playing in the bed chamber, pretending to be all different types of people with each other so that the spice and the variety continues to be a source of stimulus. The not so sensible drift from light-hearted fling to fling, not really knowing what they are looking for. The pleasure of company is the diversity of the roles you each play and the difficulty of relationship is the potential for boredom, often resulting in relationships becoming more fraternal.

Uranus in the twelfth house

The thing about the twelfth house is that it is basically indescribable. It governs everything that is nebulous, unexplained and irrational, it is the land of the unconscious and the dream. It is where fantasy rules the head and the heart, where the intuition and the sixth and seventh senses are more reliable than the logical or the feelingful. So to have the rebellious planet Uranus here is somewhat difficult because Uranus needs something to bounce off of and the vague and unformed nature of the twelfth house tends to diffuse and dissolve the more incisive and dynamic sides of Uranus.

These are the people who will always have unusual belief systems and because there are no clear boundaries or borders to give Uranus some type of framework to work with, this belief system variation can go to extremes. Here we find the absolutist or extremist, to whom everything and everyone is either yes or no, black or white with absolutely no room for compromise or flexibility. Here also can be found the complete ascetic who will live without boundaries or rules, possessions or regulatory systems and will totally go with the flow. Uranus isn't that comfortable here; it tends to revert to a default position of blissful and naive ignorance with steady plodding.

Yet in the bedchamber this can be one of the very best places for Uranus, because the lack of clear boundaries gives Uranus complete freedom to explore and develop new ideas. Most of the time these people tend to generate an easy-going, anything goes ambivalence about sex but there are danger signals here in that if they become too tolerant or flexible towards what others want without input of their own, they may suddenly find themselves in the role of suffering victim. They can live with this for a short while until it gets boring, by which time it can be difficult to extricate themselves from. These people should maintain a sense of clear boundary between them and others at least until they have had close interaction with them for a long time, because it is easy for them to get swamped by others' feelings and thus unable to either get clarity or protect themselves. Yet at the same time this is an excellent position for gentle, affectionate, sensual and compassionate love, for responding to the most subtle of signals and becoming the epitome of the empathic and intuitive lover.

The positive aspects to Uranus

When in a good mood, Uranus can be one of the most enigmatic energies in the cosmos. Uranus brings innovation as exemplified by his association with all things original, new and futuristic. He is the bit of grit in the oyster that turns into a unique pearl. Uranus thrives on the novelty, the cutting-edge excitement that brings the constant craving for active stimulation. Uranus is the ability to see round corners, to know when someone's about to say something or when something is about to happen. It has a kind of electrical feel about it that can sometimes manifest in sudden static shocks, it is not so much psychic or intuitive as much as it is cognitive and precognitive. These are the people that nothing sticks to, who seem to dance through time without it touching them. Indeed, sometimes it is as though time itself either flows a lot faster or a lot slower around them than it does for 'normal' people. Whilst they may see themselves as perfectly orthodox and conventional, their friends and community recognise the unusual and often the talented sides of their nature better than the person themselves.

Depending on their willingness to take chances (not risks but chances) these people are the trailblazers of the zodiac, the ones who open the doorways into new lands and who throw fishing lines into the future. These are the people who want nothing more than their hot and loving partner to be alongside them whilst they explore all the world has to offer.

The neutral aspects of Uranus

Uranus is different in every way. Even astronomically, its poles are on its equator so that it spins from top to bottom instead of from side to side like every other planet. It has rings at different angles to each other. It has a moon that travels in the opposite direction to its contemporaries. Uranus is the joker in the pack: it also has an element of prankster in that one can never accurately pre-empt or predict what its actions will bring. Uranus will always find the unusual way of expression, it is guaranteed to throw something extra into the mix in ways that can never quite be anticipated. Uranus represents the waves of change that periodically pass through our lives, whether they be tsunamis or just light swells.

One thing Uranus can never be accused of is being boring. Once the first signs of mundanity and embedded convention start to rear their heads Uranus will be quick to react, either by changing the dynamic and creating new energy thus circumventing the problem or by taking radical actions that dramatically changes the whole game plan. Orthodoxy, whether in the bedroom or elsewhere is the quickest way to lose these experientialists of the zodiac, so if you are partnered with one of these unusual Uranian types keep them interested by taking them somewhere they have never been before, or something equally as original and stimulating.

The difficult aspects to Uranus

Uranus used to be called the destroyer because he would always bring trouble wherever he went in your horoscope but in these more enlightened times the more challenging side of Uranus' behaviour is evident in times of sudden changes to the game plan, when out of the blue a curve ball or other form of dramatic alteration to procedure occurs, often in a momentary flash of time. Uranus has the ability and the desire to crowbar people out of routine and mundanity and the more boring or rigid the patterns are, the more disruptive the Uranian effects will be. Stubbornness or rigidity in the face of the glaring need for change can really bring life-changing and challenging problems. Sometimes there is no other alternative to just going with the flow and it makes sense to do so willingly instead of under protest and difficulty. A dominant or powerful Uranus in a chart shows a real live wire at the physical level most of the time, coupled with odd moments of complete flatness and an inability to settle into constancy or routine.

Uranus in aspect to Venus or Mars

Uranus can always be relied on to be unreliable and when aspecting Venus and/or Mars it is safe to say that this brings variation into all aspects of love and romance. It brings an energy field into your life that says to hell with mundanity and boredom, bring on the stimulus and excitement. Often people with these aspects have an eclectic bunch of friends, of varying shapes and sizes, ethnicities, genders, ages and orientations. The common link about them all is that none of them are normal and every one of them has something that makes them unique and thus acceptable to the tastes of Uranus with Mars/Venus. Sometimes these are the people that have the most unusual or unexpected careers or strange fetishes that harm no one but are more than slightly off the wall. They may have alternative lifestyles in some shape or form, have a bohemian attitude towards life and its attributes or be extremely selfish or selfless. It doesn't really matter what area of their life the difference expresses itself in as long as it is expressed. It is when the need for difference is not expressed that there can be problems and when that difference is with Venus and/or Mars, the problems can manifest in the area of personal and intimate relationship patterns.

When it comes to sex, Uranus in aspect to Venus and/or Mars is always going to have a different perspective than most. Depending on the exact nature of the interaction there can be a wide range of attitudes from puritanical celibacy to unbridled hedonism. With the difficult aspects there will be a challenge in managing and controlling sexual and sensual rhythms and there may be times of jarring and dysfunction, seemingly out of the blue. With the easier aspects there can be an openness to a number of different situations and certainly distaste for being judged on standards. One thing is crystal clear, that the link between Uranus and personal freedoms is so strong that those people with these aspects in any shape or form will never find themselves in long-term periods of boredom within their relationships. These people are catalysts, they make things happen and anyone who can't keep up with them rarely stays around for long.

Conversely, they are all good at long-term relationships but only if the magic word autonomy becomes a regular part of the interaction. It is when partners turn to each other and reaffirm that they are loved, trusted and thus free to do whatever, whenever and with whoever as long as there is honesty. Given that freedom, these people feel trusted and will rarely if ever stray. Refused that freedom and they will do the opposite of what others want just to affirm their independence.

Uranus in aspect to Venus

In today's astrological world Venus is increasingly being seen as the way in which we find and attribute value, what we find to be of worth. It is what we enjoy and derive pleasure from. Often people will have their own hierarchy of needs and values and issues such as property, food, love, hugs and cuddles, money, community and intimacy will have their place according to the nature of Venus in a person's chart. When the influence of Uranus is added into the mix it brings that added zing, edge and feeling of excitement that can be guaranteed to add spice to your life. Dependent on the nature of the aspect, Venus/Uranus contacts can bring extreme possessiveness or a renunciation of possessions, either fastidiousness or decadence and especially when young a difficulty in determining permanent value systems. Be sure if you have a strong Venus/Uranus contact in your chart that you will go through the entire range of experiences before you decide around mid-life what it is that you really want, that has value and worth and that will make you feel happy and stimulated in your later years.

In the bedroom Venus/Uranus contacts definitely bring that element of sizzle and stimulus in a way that constantly promises a degree of excitement. Even if there are no other patterns of stimulus in the chart these contacts on their own are enough to hold promise, interest and more than a hint of fun. The difficult contacts generally manifest as a commitment phobic when young and often a degree of hedonistic experimentation at least once or twice in their youth as they seek for some type of edge or boundary to the sexual experience. Constantly blowing hot and cold, they seek almost desperately to find some type of constancy in their love lives but knowing that once that constancy becomes established it quickly becomes boring and the whole cycle starts again. The flowing aspects between Venus and Uranus tend to manifest in a gentler way, often reacting well to a number of different suggestions. This is the person who will try almost anything once without fear, who has a natural curiosity about the world and who will always be interested in expanding the sensual and sexual consciousness and repertoire as long as it is consensual and fun. Venus/Uranus in almost all of its aspects has an attitude sometimes that life is too short, so when things start getting complicated they either simplify matters quickly or else prepare their exit strategy.

Uranus in aspect to Mars

The fundamental difference between Venus and Mars is that if Venus is what you want and enjoy then Mars is the way that you get it. Mars is the assertive, projective and dynamic of the two and when coupled with the electrical and radical energy of Uranus there can be and often is an edge to your life that sets you apart from the majority of others. A challenging aspect between Mars and Uranus creates such a high energetic output that unless well managed it can result in radical, rash, headstrong and impulsive actions born out of boredom and spontaneity which will almost always end up with bumps, bangs, bruises or even injuries. It creates a very physical lifestyle where actions always speak louder than words and life is for living to the max. It is sometimes accompanied by the capacity for incisive and on the spot decision making.

The more complimentary aspects between Mars and Uranus will manifest in a less extreme way but still carry in them the capacity for spontaneous action, albeit not in such a shocking or disruptive way as those with the challenging aspects. The flowing aspects bring with them the willingness to try anything that offers new experience and that can create a new sense of stimulus.

As far as the more intimate side of life goes, this is a very highly charged combination. There often will be a highly charged libido and because this is Mars and not Venus that need for expression will be demonstrated quite clearly into the world. There will be the need for an active sex life and those with the flowing aspects should find that this area of their life is one of regular surprise in a beneficial way with various degrees of healthy variation leading to an active, stimulating and interesting love life. The challenging aspects also have this capacity but they are also often accompanied by an urgency for expression that can sometimes ride roughshod over other people's feelings and sensitivities. They can be sexual dynamos but also have a low attention and boredom threshold so often tire of environments quite quickly. To some of these people, physical stimulus is the Holy Grail.

Uranus sextile Venus or Mars

In the contemporary astrological world, the meaning of a sextile between two planets in a person's chart is increasingly being seen as the aspect of opportunity involving the work ethic of the harder aspects but also the growth potential of the easier ones. When Uranus is involved the sextile of opportunity is going to be seen as an active area of development hopefully leading to stimulus, innovation and originality within the voluntary confines of your personal and intimate relationship patterns.

With Uranus sextile Venus there will always be the desire to get on with a wide and eclectic range of people united by a cognisance of individuality and a dislike of the insincere. There is normally an innate willingness to flow with the go and to synchronise intuitively with the vibe around yourself at any given time and to make the most of it. By doing this you naturally and organically dance with the communal and futuristic energy of the future, something this aspect is well tuned into. There is a need for occasional space even in the best of relationships and provided that space is given freely it is rarely taken. A willing and tolerant acceptance of the more unusual attitudes is common, normally leading to enjoyable intimate experiences based on voluntary interdependence. This aspect often brings an element of giggling and wide-eyed adventure into the intimate side of life, an interesting degree of fun-filled variation into the sexual experience (often involving futuristic and Uranian gadgetry) and a flexibility and tolerance towards anything except dishonesty.

With the sextile between Uranus and Mars the energy exchange is more dynamic. There will be an active enthusiasm towards life, a kind of 'get up and go' attitude that normally works and is never boring, as well as an innovative strategy for life based on individual skills and talents in a way that eventually can become highly specialised if somewhat unconventional and sometimes misunderstood. Once the conscious recognisance of choosing to live within your own boundaries as opposed to fighting against others is realised life becomes a veritable dynamo of concentrated and focussed energetic output that takes into account the needs of the community and the future as much, if not more so, than the immediate needs of yourself. Because the sextile is based on opportunity, the favourable blend of Mars and Uranus does recognise other people's needs as well and is comfortable about working in mutual tandem providing it is not too clinging. The Martian need for independence and individuality will extend into the bedroom and there will be a friendly competitiveness that will involve lots of tickling, giggling and game/role playing in equal turn and measure. Mars/Uranus needs the façade of freedom even in-long term personal and intimate partnerships and often fantasizes or dreams but only acts when really bored. They don't stray as long as there is a constancy and novelty to their existing love life.

Uranus trine Venus or Mars

The trine aspect is more latent than the sextile. It links two planetary energies that are in the same element and creates a natural and organic flow of consistency and pleasure as well as a Uranian disregard for the conventions of modern society.

With Venus being the more social as opposed to Mars being the more active the trine between Uranus and Venus suggests that the company you keep will be seen as different and stimulating if somewhat idiosyncratic and there will be a common thread of humanitarianism. There can be the tendency to become involved in future looking groups whether organised or social, although beware the temptation to get into routines. In intimate relationships there will be an ease of expression when it comes to the sexual and sensual sides of life but there is a need for your lover to first and foremost be a friend because once possessiveness becomes part of the equation there will be problems. If Venus trine Uranus feels in any way constrained or limited by the relationship the first instinct is going to be to talk about it, bring it up and try and sort it out. Only if this doesn't work does the famed 'plan B' of the quick exit strategy rear its ugly head. These people generally tend to have an open, honest and refreshing approach to sex. It's only when complications set in that they start turning off.

Uranus trine Mars has a more proactive feel to it. It often manifests as high physical output, athletic ability, manual dexterity and a willingness to utilise the body as effectively and efficiently as possible, to live life to the full and to maximise the opportunities that life brings. A combination of powerful vitality and energy with a healthy creative output does make for a stimulating and normally active lifestyle, although in order for this creativity to be fully realised there is also a need for a steady and consistent amount of self-discipline. There will be a strong sexual element to the relationship and an openness to variety and experimentation with a resistance to the sex on a Friday night, two point two kids, mortgage and car and job lifestyle. At the same time providing there is trust there will never be the need to wander. There will be a fondness for the al fresco lifestyle and the idea of running naked through nature will always have a highly charged sexual connotation to it. Provided one is partnered with a physical equal there will be a hugely fulfilling sex life.

Uranus square Venus or Mars

The square between Venus and Uranus can manifest in a number of different ways, with the emphasis being firmly placed on the word 'different'. There will always be a shortage of patience with the mundane and the conventional and there will also always be a corresponding search for that something different which these people think will fulfil them. This ongoing and constant search for the right type of stimulus that they think they are looking for eventually comes to a dead end, at which point they realise that they create their own reality and that they are responsible for their way of seeing things. If they never find this point of internal acceptance they will always look to others for answers, ultimately leading to a hedonistic and unfulfilling lifestyle and quick burn out. There will always be a sporadic element to the sexual energy, sometimes being completely passive and other times being totally dominant and there will be a need for flexibility and understanding on the part of the partner, who themselves need to have an open and experimental attitude towards sex and relationships. Often two people with this aspect come together, recognising in each other the freedom that they individually crave.

The square from Uranus to Mars can be much more volatile and disruptive. Sometimes it's almost as if they are looking for a fight, or at least a cause. There is a deep passion, a questing and searching for some type of noble cause that is worth putting effort into and this can and often does ride roughshod over other people's sensitivities. There can be a crusader mentality where it is me/us against the world, with the desire to stridently stand up for your beliefs. Mars square Uranus creates an electrical energy around yourself that can powerfully and magnetically both repulse and attract at the same instant.

There is a need with this aspect to steadily gain a greater control of physical energy, ideally through some form of martial arts practice and if trained properly this degree of finesse can translate into the bedroom and become finely tuned to a degree of sophistication rarely seen. In order to get there, the amount of almost monk-like discipline needed can sometimes be too much, throwing the individual back into the world of temporary but vivid sensation and the ability for many different forms of sexual development and experience. Sex should not be used as an anaesthetic or derided in other ways, it should be remembered that it is a pleasure as much as, if not more than, a function.

Uranus opposite Venus

To an extent, this combination depends on the gender of the signs and houses that it occupies. For example, if Venus is in a feminine sign there will be a lot of pouting and preening, the sending of signals and the active playing of the game whereas if Venus is in a masculine sign then there will be a much more proactive way of dealing with things, often involving direct and to the point conversations and actions. This aspect emphasises the need for freedom from commitment in relationship patterns at least until well into the thirties. Uranus will constantly revolutionise and stimulate the Venusian value system, leading to a lot of changing of mind, opinion, attraction and feeling.

The first half of life is generally a time of experimentation and experience in a number of different arenas with the end result that they find out by the age of forty what it is that they don't want, which is a long way down the road to working out what they do want. It may well be that after half a lifetime of fighting for their independence and freedom they come to the realisation that what they really want is a home and a family. However, it has to be them that makes that realisation and if it is forced upon them, they will run away. This is the 'kiss me quick' aspect of sudden falling in love over your fifth glass of wine, of instantaneous attraction normally followed fairly rapidly (at least when young) by developing boredom and the urge for freedom. Strangely enough, when the sensible ones with this aspect (that is, the ones who wait until later in life) partner down, they generally do so in a way that will then be consistent, content and fun. Firstly, they have to be clear with themselves what it is that they actually want and sometimes that really can take many years.

Uranus opposite Mars

So what happens when the two most volatile, feisty and independent forces in the entire zodiac end up opposing each other in someone's chart? Well for a substantial part of the person's life, fireworks. This really can be the anarchic rebel without a cause, the tinderbox looking for an explosion to ignite and the desire to transform society through some 'moment of change'. There can be a rejection of the conventional and orthodox and sometimes the embracing of specific forms of fundamentalism. Yet at the same time this aspect is found to be common in the charts of different types of engineers, whether structural, genetic, nuclear, architectural or otherwise. The idea of large power systems and the transformation of power is a basic inherent talent.

If these people choose to work with their physical energy in a disciplined and focussed way they can become as sharp as there is. These are the metaphorical black belts of the zodiac and once they learn the secret of self-empowerment through attention, focus and discipline they become unstoppable, the cyber warrior monks of the future. Translate this energy into the bedroom and it immediately becomes clear that this is no ordinary energy. People with Mars opposite Uranus will either be strangely passive, almost scared to be assertive in which case there may be deeper pathological issues or much more likely they will be extremely lively and proactive, playing their partner almost like a musical instrument. They may experience sex in a more mechanical way than many but that's not better or worse, just different and being different really suits these radical but strangely hip troublemakers.

Uranus conjunct Venus

Venus can somewhat crudely be summed up as what it is that turns you on and when Venus is together with Uranus the answer will be almost anything as long as it is interesting and definitely not boring. These are the people who travel to far off lands and have romantic interludes that they remember with a smile in their minds for the rest of their lives. They may be quite conventional themselves but the second they see their friends getting into a rut it's out with the crowbar and on with the tap of excitement. They are always doing something and their social life can often be quite hectic. Unconventional value systems, both in areas of home/family as well as relationship patterns, can be common and these people like their partners to be equally self-empowered. This aspect can be the spirit of adventure and it can bring the joy of life to the fore.

Depending on the sign and house position that Venus and Uranus occupy, the attitude towards intimacy can vary tremendously. There will always be the need for personal freedom within the confines of the relationship and as long as this is acknowledged then this position gives a fun-loving and open attitude towards sex with a willingness to try anything that is pleasurable and that brings a mutual glow to the occasion. The wise ones with this position know that the best way for them to get maximum pleasure is to ensure that their partner is also having a good time and that the best forms of intimacy are those that involve lots of eye contact and laughter.

Uranus conjunct Mars

This is an electrical powerhouse with static emerging at times, a dynamo that can both catalyse and destroy, sometimes at the same time. These people can combine the raw energy of Mars and the futuristic tendencies of Uranus together and project forwards into the future with a degree of innovation and inspiration not usually found elsewhere. It gives unusual energetic output sometimes seemingly running on a different current stream than the rest of humanity and it brings the ability to metaphorically dance with time. Sometimes time does seem to either speed up or slow down around these people and there is often a strong capacity for sudden precognition. There will be strong stamina and drive coupled with isolated moments of complete meltdown, often only for ten minutes. Their need for independence, liberty and freedom at all costs especially when young can lead them into areas that when older they might shudder to remember.

These are the risk takers of the zodiac, the shock wave futurists who instigate and innovate before quickly moving on, leaving fertile growth behind them for others to pick up on. This energy obviously makes it hard for people with this aspect to settle down into long-term relationships at least until older because the world has so much to offer and they have so much energy to spend. They can often channel the more physical or raw side of their nature into something specific that speaks of higher development, such as Tantra, higher forms of yoga, anything that elevates the sexual experience into a kind of electrical bliss. They will be sporadic in the bedroom at times as the current alternates and the on/off switch changes. It can be quite raw in its expression if not managed wisely which is why many with this aspect turn to some form of self-mastery as they age, often resulting in them becoming consummate and highly skilled lovers.

12

Neptune

The fantasy, imagination and mystery of love

Neptune is by its nature a mystery to us. It is one of the transpersonal planets, far away in the heavens and invisible to the naked eye. As far as is known, Neptune is primarily a mixture of methane and other gases that form a light electric blue cloud cover which occasionally breaks to reveal tantalising glimpses of white light from underneath. According to ancient Greek mythology, Neptune was present at the fall of his father, Cronos (Saturn) and the resulting sharing of the Earth's domains amongst his sons. Zeus (Jupiter) took the overworld and sky kingdoms as his own whilst Hades (Pluto) took the underworld for his domain. Neptune, in his Greek guise of Poseidon, took on the domain of the waters. Since time immemorial Neptune has been associated with the seas and oceans. The cloud covering the planets body is indicative of the nebulous and opaque nature of its deep-sea resonance. Wherever Neptune is in your horoscope by aspect and by house position shows where the capacity for both mystery and illumination lie, along with the equally opposite attributes of escapism and addiction alongside and parallel with clarity and spirituality.

The house positions of Neptune

Although any interpretation of Neptune by house will be influenced by its aspects from other planets, as far as the 'real' world goes Neptune by house position shows where you can inspire yourself to the highest of highs and where you can drag yourself into the lowest of lows. It is where you can take the initial input of vision, dream and imagination and slowly turn it into applied reality through some type of creativity that carries intuition as well as effort and it is also where you can be conned by the world or by other(s), either unwittingly, or even worse knowingly, but unable to escape that pattern.

As far as the sexual and sensual goes, Neptune is the doorway to a wonderland of potential fantasy and play. Every house position of Neptune will have its own little fetish and quirk where it can dream and play, safe within the confines of the bedroom. Neptune is where you can find the really kinky (although not the dominant or powerful side of that element of sexuality, instead the more exotic and sensual), given to pleasurable experience through some type of blissful existence. Here is where you find the sexual perfectionist, aspiring to an ever-higher degree of consciousness through their sexual and sensual practices. Here also you can find the flagrant hedonist who will try anything once and most things twice and if it involves some form of extravagance and sensual expansion, so much the better. Sometimes also found is the celibate, choosing not to experience pleasures of the flesh and instead transmuting that energy into a higher form of consciousness.

Neptune in the first house

The first house is generally associated with your personality, identity, sense of individuality, physical and often facial characteristics and your way of being projective and assertive in the outside world. Neptune here usually brings a quality of empathy rarely found in others, making the individual periodically ultra-sensitive to the energy fields around them. Whilst Neptune in the first house brings a more subtle appreciation of the artistic, spiritual and emotive experiences in the world, as well as a personal aura of enigmatic and mysterious charm, it can also lead to considerable potential for either self-delusion or else deliberately blurring boundaries between you and others so that you don't have to deal with absolutes. This process in time leads to a dissolving of your own sense of identity as you try to be all things to all people instead of being yourself, nebulous though that concept may seem. Sometimes the opposite side of being impressionable is the state of being intuitive and as long as you are not clouding your systems through excessive toxins, your intuitive gut instinct is always going to be a good guide. There is a regular need to reinforce self-imagery and see yourself as an individual, lest the world absorb or consume you with listlessness and a lack of direction becomes the end result.

Neptune in the first house in the bedroom is where the realm of the true dreamer and fantasist lies. The first house is quintessentially about the relationship that you have with yourself at all levels but especially physically in terms of your drive and vivacity. Neptune here brings both the nebulous all giving slave to affection and the king/queen in their castle ruling over their subjects. This position will sometimes literally bend over backwards to please you in the bedroom but when the fancy takes them you had better do what they want or else there is going to be trouble. Part of them loves being the slave, playing the game of helplessness at various different levels, it's all to do with that Neptunian secret desire for ultimate surrender and dissolution. At other times they can indulge themselves by playing the role of being the master or mistress, safe in the knowledge that the role playing exists only in the bedroom. There can occasionally be a light element of sado-masochism here but only if the other planetary aspects, particularly to Venus and/or Mars, are in challenging shape. The easiest thing for these people to do in the bed chamber is to step into the land of fantasy knowing that issues of surrender and dominance can be safely explored and confined within those walls. The hardest thing here is to maintain the middle ground and not let yourself go to extremes. Neptune in the first house can take you to heaven or it can take you to hell, as long as you remember that you have the choice.

Neptune in the second house

The second house is normally associated with issues of value and worth and how they appear in the outside world. Consequently, this normally manifests as financial affairs, property, possessions, assets and your own sense of inner stability and solidity, finding worth through the world in yourself. There is often a confusing attitude towards money, in that you can make it but as for keeping hold of it... There is a need to bring a degree of structure and responsibility into your financial situations, or else things can get nebulous and confusing fast because Neptune in this position often denotes an unwillingness to look objectively and rationally at your own finances. At the same time there can just as easily be a 'devil may care' attitude around money, living for today and not tomorrow.

The insecure types with this position will squirrel caches of money around the house whilst the more mature types will understand that it is not quantity that really has value but quality. If there is a more non materialistic philosophy to life, then perhaps independent financial advice and management is recommended. Yet somehow, nine times out of ten this position has the fortunate knack of manifesting exactly what it is that they need at just the right time.

Because of its association with Taurus, the second house has the essence of value at its prime centre and when blended with a combination of Neptune and sex it can be the playground for a number of different sexual and sensual experiences. This is the person who needs to be told that they are loved and valued. The less spiritually aware will seek that bedroom value by having dollar bills or pound notes attached to their bed linen, whilst the more spiritually aware will not be caught up totally in the prison of flesh and will instead find value through experience and sensation as much as, if not more than, material reward.

For some strange reason, the more kinky and adventurous of these people like to experiment with slippery foodstuffs, particularly things like yoghurt or honey that can easily be licked off. Even when the sexual temperature is temporarily down, these are the people who will quite happily use your naked body as a plate for their more exotic meals, bringing both themselves and you unusual pleasure and stimulus. If there is a problem here it is in their apparent inability to know when to stop. Neptune in the second house can have the attitude that you can never have too much of a good thing and as a result blatant hedonism can occur, often as the doorway to a level of depravity and consumption that would normally appal you. You really can enjoy your sex life with this position as long as you know when to stop.

Neptune in the third house
The third house relates to your immediate environment and your ability to communicate in and through it. It can denote an intuitive and receptive

mind but discernment is the key to keeping things clear, or else daydreaming and vagueness can become a strong part of your mental faculties. The third house is where you think and talk to others, so the best principle with Neptune in this house is the philosophy that if you always tell the truth then you never have to remember what you have said. You can't make rigid rules here because Neptune will dissolve them if you do but you can learn to surf the intuitive edges and be selective as to what you believe until you have seen proof. Visualization techniques are recommended as well as a relatively flexible schedule that isn't regular and rigid, although a regularly updated diary is strongly advised. There is a degree of charm here that makes other people eager to learn from you because they can sense that you can blend fact with intuition and create something artistic from the resulting words but be careful to always keep things as simple and transparent as you can because once things get foggy then confusion can easily set in.

The inherent nature of the third house is that of communication, primarily with words. These are the people who will have a number of different secret personas buried in their private spaces, waiting for opportunities to express themselves and they will play different characters in the bedroom, depending on their mood. They can be so, so flirtatious with you on the one hand but you better let them know that you appreciate it quickly, because the fickle side of this position is not known for its patience and if not pampered or at least acknowledged from the word go this Neptune position finds it easier to move on than almost any other. To keep them, whisper in their ears in different accents and wear things that take them a long time to undo. They all seem to have a lurid capacity for description and they can tell the best dirty stories in the zodiac if they know that they have got a receptive audience. Neptune involves the imagination and the third house uses information and words to communicate that imagination, hence the funny accents, the erotic stories and innovative use of the tongue. These are the people who will lick you or suck you anywhere as long as they can still talk to you at the same time and what they can't do with their tongue they will do with their fingers, especially if it involves tickling. Insatiably curious of everything about you, they are looking for someone to worship but you better listen to them and play their game otherwise they will find you boring and quickly move on.

Neptune in the fourth house

The fourth house represents the home, roots and foundations. This can be materially in terms of bricks and mortar, emotionally in terms of the relationship you had with your parents and privately where you nurture others and hopefully allow others to nurture you. You may have one of the parents on a pedestal or one of the parents may have had high ideals, strong compassion or the opposite, escapism and avoidance. There may be a degree of uncertainty or confusion about childhood and if so, you may find your nurturing needs outside of the blood family. There can occasionally be isolationist tendencies with this position so remember with this that you live in a human body with physical needs. Certainly the home needs to be a place of comfort and ease where one can just sink into the sofa or the bath. If you have Neptune in the fourth house then at the end of the day you are probably never going to make clear lucid sense of your past. You can sense, guess, envision, dream, intuit and know in a non-logical way but as soon as you try to understand it slips away like sand through your fingers so instead of worrying about the past, focus on making your current residence your true home.

It is in the bedroom where we find the true romanticists and fantasists of the zodiac, at least as far as playing at mummy and daddy goes. Neptune likes to weave a web and in the bed chamber that web can be one of protection, nurturing, hugs, cuddles and affection in a way that sometimes comes dangerously close to becoming parent-child. As with all things Neptunian there is nothing wrong with this type of behaviour as long as you know that you are doing it (or being done to). The likely worst-case scenario of this position is that of one partner wearing diapers or sucking dummies, although admittedly this is an extreme. This is certainly an evocative position. People here can love and hate in equal measure and sometimes it doesn't matter which feeling is being demonstrated as long as there is a depth of emotion to it that can be not only related to and felt but lived and experienced to the hilt.

The fourth house is the conduit whereby other people's emotional influences can be felt at their most powerful and all these people secretly want to do is be wanted by their partner. Perhaps their greatest single fear is that of abandonment or being unwanted and they can go to any lengths including total surrender in order to keep their partner. Sadly this rarely works unless there is mutual dependency and even then things can get messy. Sexually, the fourth house Neptune position needs to rotate between being the child, the parent and the equal, mature, adult partner.

Neptune in the fifth house

The fifth house is the area of creativity, procreativity, children, fun and games, romance and pleasurable forms of speculation and Neptune here adds a quality of inspiration, almost theatrical ability and certainly a strong sense of drama. This combination can amplify your creative nature as well as emphasise your more romantic and whimsical side. It brings the desire for courting, wooing, chocolate and flowers, all the attributes of romance as opposed to steady relationship. If you have Neptune here you are likely to find that your relationships with young children provide you with a great deal of both pleasure and inspiration. There can also be artistic or musical talent as Neptune here stimulates the creative centres and enables you to reach out for stimulation. It can also lead to disillusion if you are not careful as this is one of the two main positions where people fall in love rather than just being in love. It is also not uncommon for these individuals to have unrealistic expectations of their children, so remember to let your kids have their fun whilst they are young enough to do so and don't put too much expectation on them.

In the bedroom, this is the position where the inner child really comes out to play and it doesn't matter really in what context the sensual, sexual and intimate sides of life come out as long as there is an element of playfulness and childlike qualities. Childlike, not childish. This is the position of the eternal youth regardless of physical age and there is a part of these people that constantly sees themselves as Adonis or Aphrodite, the epitome of perfection in the opposite gender's eyes. They truly are Marlon Brando or Judy Garland, the ultimate fantasy figure at least in their own eyes and there is always a small part of them that's truly astonished that the rest of the world doesn't see them that way. They will take a delight in exploring every part of you, body and soul but you are in big, big trouble if you don't return the compliment twofold.

These are the people who need devotees, who need to hear that they are the apple of your eye and that you couldn't possibly live without them at least for that moment of time. They love the resplendent. A four-poster with a mirror tile ceiling will do if there is nothing else and here they share the same quality as their Leonine cousins in that they know that it's hard to be modest when you know you are the best and if the outside world, often represented by the partner or ex-partner, doesn't recognise it, that's their problem, there are always new horizons to be explored and other people to make these Hollywood fantasists feel special.

Neptune in the sixth house

The sixth house is the area of work, service, duty and responsibility for those less fortunate than yourself, as well as being strongly associated with health, hygiene and diet/nutrition. It is the area of your lifestyle management routine. There is a philosophy here that says that if your efforts in life benefit others as much as, if not more than, yourself then you will always be successful. Neptune here brings a few challenges, as well as a few gifts. There may be the occasional need for personal sacrifice and certainly most toxins should be kept at a distance. A sensitivity to environment and the energy of people around can have a stronger than average effect on physical well-being and energy levels, so a healthy and steady nutritional regime is recommended, i.e. no fasting!

There will be a strong desire to help those less fortunate or less able than yourself, so standing up and speaking for children, the elderly, the disadvantaged or disabled, animals or nature will always feature in your life. There is a need for the establishment of a regular routine so that there is something consistent in your life that can be relied on, because otherwise boundaries become so nebulous that you will inadvertently get sucked dry or absorbed by others.

As far as the sexual and sensual sides of life go, this is probably the hardest position for Neptune to find itself in. The sixth house persona desperately wants to feel accepted by other or others and as a result will do almost anything to feel part of a team and thus not isolated, and in this desire for belonging they can sow the seeds of their own destruction. There can be an almost pathological desire to be needed, so much so that they will change everything about themselves in order to fit with the supposed ideals of their significant other, only to find that this adaptation is the very thing that drives that significant other away. These needy people can turn into sexual predators within the confines of a consensual bedroom where they let their wider fantasy life emerge safely, whilst at the other end of the spectrum they can get an almost obsessive pleasure from playing the victim, begging for mercy, release, pleasure or any combination of these and other sensations.

There is a need in all of these individuals to realise and then remember that fantasy normally stays between the ears and the only way that it can safely emerge in the bedroom is through mutual and consensual practice. The imagination, however, can be created and here is where the dream leaves the bedroom and goes out into the world. These people can ooze sex like a stick in a kind of wide-eyed innocent way or they can be the biggest victims on the block and either is OK as long as they know that they are doing it.

Neptune in the seventh house

The seventh house is the area of your chart that deals with all forms of one-to-one relationship, whether family, friend, social, professional or personal and intimate. When Neptune is here there can often be the search for the perfect partner or soul mate, with the standard response to this being that this magical person is probably alive now but ninety-eight years old and living in a cave in the Himalayas, or just born in the Amazon rain forest. These spiritually lonely souls crave the intimacy of partnership but too many times this is projected into dependency where the individual becomes addicted to the relationship, only seeing the partner's good sides instead of reality, often leading to disappointment. There is a conscious need for objectivity in all relationship patterns to avoid negative repetition and self-defeatism.

The idealism and unrealistic attitude towards inappropriate people, symbolised by "Oh, she'll/he'll change" is their undoing and in the outside world there is a tendency to always think the best of everybody. As long as this is done with a degree of both caution and acceptance there will be no problem but beware of becoming the dumping ground for other people's problems. Yet, when you find someone whom you can work and be with over a number of years, a sense of organic and empathic appreciation grows to become a permanent relationship of strength and consistency. The key to this position is that in order to have good working relationships with other people at the one-to-one level, you need to project that quality you are looking for in others out into the world, on the grounds that like attracts like.

The blue-eyed idealists of the zodiac, these are the ones who hold their intimate partners and their relationships with them at the forefront of their consciousness. To them the idea of being single can be so depressing that the lower evolved of these people will do anything for their partners to avoid rejection. Of course, in time most of these will realise that in order to be in a good relationship with anyone else you first of all have to be in a good relationship with yourself, otherwise you enter relationships at a disadvantage from the word go thus attracting insubstantial people.

There can be a tendency with this position to put their partners on pedestals, to only see their good sides and be blissfully ignorant of their less attractive qualities. Yet at the same time, when teamed up with someone as sensitive and receptive as themselves these gentle souls can prove to be so understanding and tolerant of their partner that they become idyllic relationship material. Never, ever lie to them because that is the cardinal sin for these trusting folk and their carefully constructed world could easily come tumbling down if they are being deceived. They need to feel that they can trust in order to fully love, yet when they can commit to trust there is no other position in the zodiac that is so dedicated to their relationship. They will go along with any type of action in the bedroom as long as it's not too deviant, although they all secretly want to play damsels in distress and knights in shining armour.

Neptune in the eighth house

The eighth house is associated with external funds, whether partners' money, joint resources, inheritance, tax rebate, sponsorship, loans or any other type of financial or material input. The eighth house also has a strong association with the darker and potentially more fearful sides of life, as represented by the rawness of the sexual experience and the inevitability of death. If you find that your financial life often goes through periods of dissolving or confusion, then perhaps there is a need for you to take firmer control of the reins out of the hands of others, lest things become blurred. If you keep transparent and regular accounts and all agreements written down in clear black and white then things will never get confusing.

This position often brings a greater understanding to the death transition process than average and these individuals are often found providing either neonatal or palliative care. In fact, they are so sensitive to the consequences of age that if they are not involved in something that deeply benefits and transforms others' lives there can be a lack of purpose or even unfulfillment which can at times lead to despair and isolationist tendencies.

The sexual element of the eighth house is one of the most misunderstood of positions. Many people still think of the eighth primarily as the house of sex and death, whilst the reality of the situation is that there is far more to this than meets the eye. It is the area of the psychological, the insightful, the mysterious and the hidden and in these contexts Neptune is quite comfortable in this area. The quasi Scorpionic nature of the eighth house fits well with Neptune's love of the more nebulous and esoteric. Neptune is rarely going to go all the way in the eighth house, it is normally content to just simmer and pout, to tantalize and promise, to be a figure of mystery and allure but without the teasing that can sometimes really wind people up.

People with Neptune in the eighth are going to be very good at subtly coercing you into revealing your deepest and most private sides but God help you if you go nosing too deeply into their personal lives. They can be quite secretive about their personal nature but this is normally to disguise the fact that they often don't have that much of a sex life once you are past the mystique, or at least until you have known them intimately for at least seven years, because it can take them that long to really trust someone. They secretly love the idea of taking risks and flirting with danger and exposure but for most of them an active fantasy life is as far as it gets, although those that choose knowingly to develop the imagination can become the most intuitive and passionate of lovers and end up really contented as long as they ensure that they get as much as they give.

Neptune in the ninth house

The ninth house is generally associated with the higher sides of life through expanding your experience, knowledge and consciousness. When young this is often done through anthropological travel and active cultural participation and when older through higher minded education or teaching. The ninth house also has to do with the higher forms of law, publishing, teaching, religion, philosophy and ultimately wisdom. It's easy with this position to have big dreams, to see how the world can be. When it comes to living it in a practical way, there can be a degree of disappointment when you realise that the ideal is only a fleeting glimpse, not the permanent reality. There can be the desire to transcend the harshness of reality through some type of self-development that takes you out of yourself (for example yoga, meditation, Buddhism) into a more philosophical space. The more you look outside yourself for answers, the greater the potential for the zealot or fundamentalist. There should be caution in believing the truths of others yet an acceptance of their right to disagree with you. This acceptance of others leads to a greater relationship within yourself with divinity and the universe, creating a beautiful quality of faith in the future with openness to new concepts and belief systems. Just keep one foot on the ground.

Also here we find the knights in shining armour rescuing damsels in distress, or the warrior princess liberating her people. These are the dreamers of the zodiac and when transposed into the bedroom this position brings a great deal of aspiration and humour into your love making techniques and skills. At the same time this position can create a degree of unreality in hopes and wishes, either pushing too hard or expecting too much from others. There can always be the difficulty in separating the dream from the real, although the sensible ones learn over time that they can project that fantasy image onto their partner warts and all and find true love not in the appearance or the passion as much as in the intelligence and the aspirations.

These are the people who want to have sex in every possible position in every possible location, preferable outdoors in nature. The ones with this position who fail to find contentment with themselves and their partners will always look for something or someone better, although that 'better' perpetually remains a vague impression in the indiscernible future and commitment will remain a foreign land. With Neptune in the ninth, it is a mating of the higher minds as much as it is a union of the physical bodies and only when the two actively combine together in something that is clean, transparent and humorous does this position work to its best capacity. There is an increasing emphasis on the more subtle and sensual as opposed to the sexual as you age.

Neptune in the tenth house

Most commonly associated with career, work and job, the tenth house also deals with authority whether parent, God, taxman or employer. It also has a lot to do with your public image and the way you project yourself into the world as being. Neptune here can bring confusion into your goals and ambitions but at the same time can provide a genuinely aspirational career that benefits many other people as much as, if not more than, yourself. There can be recognition for your work but if not properly structured there can also be spectacular falls from grace.

Neptune here normally gives a good intuition and recognition of coming trends and perhaps sometimes you just have to trust that intuitive side of yourself when uncertainty about professional domain ensues. Regardless of whether you are prominent in your position in the world or not, make sure that the outside world is under no misapprehension about who you are or what you stand for. Your ability to be a 'cool hunter' or trend setter keeps you one step ahead of the bunch much of the time, even though sometimes it's a lonely place. Don't let yourself become the head of a bandwagon or cause unless you truly believe in what you are doing.

In the bedroom, Neptune in the tenth is where we find the uptight, rigid and inflexible disciplinarian as well as the ultimate hedonist. This is not a position of moderation or mundanity; whichever way you look at it Neptune in the tenth house has a kinky side to its nature. These are the people who will experiment with light bondage from both sides of the equation, or they will wear tight clothing, whether it is basques or garters but only underneath: the outside world can't possibly know, because the mortification and shame would be unbearable. In their fantasies they live a double life being prim and proper on the outside and either a raver or a frump on the inside and some of them actually take those fantasies into their real lives, so you never can tell with this position what you will get until you cautiously dip your toe in the water.

These people need a partner who will alternate between being the helpless one and the master/mistress and although there are echoes of mummy and daddy here, it's more to do with ideas and actions of authority, strength and surrender rather than domesticity or family patterns. Of course, the association of the tenth house with fame and prominence brings out the glamorous, beautiful and sometimes garish side of this position, where sometimes their exalted social status makes them unapproachable by mere mortals, quickly leading to aloofness and ultimately loneliness. All the world's a stage and the people merely players but these dreamers are their own casting directors...

Neptune in the eleventh house

The eleventh house is all about community: it is your friends, your clubs and associations and it is how you deal with people on the street and society at large. It has a lot to do with your long-term wishes and dreams, although the more they have a humanitarian tinge the more likely they are to come true. The desire to help those less fortunate is strong here and as long as you don't surrender it all you will find the more that you give, the more you have got to give. Remember that you do things in community for the benefit of the group not for individuals, otherwise you just get taken for granted, so a degree of discernment is asked of you here. You do things for others because you want to, for no other reason and with clear boundaries. Through this philosophy you find groups and friends who become as close, if not closer, than family and once they have been around seven years, they will normally stay good forever. So be selective of and patient with community and you will find that as time evolves so they become all you could ask for in friends. Yet at the same time don't dissolve yourself entirely into community, because you can lose your sense of individuality if you do. Remember to keep some 'me' time.

On the surface Neptune in the eleventh house people are the popular, attractive and generally amenable types that you can experience at the day by day level all the time and indeed if you have this position there is going to be an element of experiencing your friends and local community as being really close. Underlying this genteel position at the emotional level lies a heart of solid steel and when crossed these people become as cold as a fridge, often permanently as well. It is hard to fall out with them but it's even harder to regain their trust when offended. Because they are naturally affectionate at the superficial level, everyone falls in love with them at first glance making it difficult to dislike these people with a strange glint in their eye. All of the social and communicative life can act as a distraction from the relationship they have with their bodies and the physical side of life can sometimes come second when the social and community life comes calling. They can be random in their quest for affection and emotion, almost boundary-less, and to them other people's morals or scruples can sometimes just be seen as examples of their own narrow-mindedness. More than any other position, Neptune in the eleventh house is clear about the difference between sex and emotion, about how the former can be almost just a necessary bodily function whilst the latter takes years of development and growth. Their partners need to be their friends as much as their lovers.

Neptune in the twelfth house

This area presents the unconscious self, the subconscious impulses and the imaginative faculties and is the area of the intuitive and the artist in us all. It is the land of the dream and as a result these people tend to be more comfortable with their own company than most other positions and often spend times in their lives alone, either by choice or otherwise. One side of the coin is the introspective nature, which can lead into escapist tendencies such as alcohol, religion, narcotics etc… This is opposed by the deep compassion the individual feels for the world's suffering.

Over the course of a life, Neptune here tends to evolve from escapist behaviour when young into artistic, humanitarian and spiritual development when older. There is a boundless faith that normally runs deep but when needed is invulnerable. Although the desire to work with less well-off people is strong, care should be taken in order not to soak up negativity from others otherwise they become addicted to you leaving you drained and exhausted. With Neptune in the twelfth, one person's daydream or fantasy can be another's creative imagination and the difference is your willingness to keep at least one foot solidly rooted in the here and now in order to avoid cycles of disappointment.

As far as the bedroom goes Neptune is in its element, able to surf the waves of love and life without really understanding the process behind the experience. To these sensual and sensitive people sex and sensuality are some of the ways of achieving that bliss they all secretly aspire to. They are capable of just grasping the moment and of using the physical experience as a vehicle for an almost transcendent elevation in consciousness and the sensible ones amongst them know that to share that sensuality with their partners heightens their own experience. One touch, one word or look at the right time can carry the most erotically charged symbolism to these sensual sponges, so obviously they need to maintain a degree of protection around themselves lest they become the archetypal twelfth house victim or martyr, conning yourself or being deceived by others. Given the right partner and the right time they can play their lover's body like a finely tuned instrument, raising them both to sensual heights normally unattainable. This is not normally the position for the course, for the rough and tumble, instead these people like to think of themselves as sexual sophisticates or else as celibates, not lowering themselves to the pleasures of the flesh.

The beautiful thing is that most of the time these sensitive souls don't even know what they are doing, they are just tuning into that subconscious vibe and it just develops around them but there is Neptune in the twelfth house for you.

The positive aspects to Neptune

There is the easy way and then there is the not so easy way and with Neptune you can never really tell which is which until it is too late. At its highest form, Neptune really is the planet most commonly associated with spirituality. It is where words like intuition, imagination and creativity work with other concepts such as illumination and enlightenment. Neptune can truly represent the relationship and the interaction that you have with the Divine, however you choose to conceive the Divine as being. It is where the ability to bring structure into the imagination can produce great works of art, as well as where you can inspire yourself to ever greater feats or aspirations involving you walking your talk or having faith and belief in what you are doing to the point of positive inspiration.

Neptune is where you become more poetic as opposed to logical. It represents your capacity for intuitive knowledge beyond any rational sureness and can create the 'walking psychic sponge' effect where the capacity for empathy is so strong that it can at times swamp the individual in a way that makes clarity sometimes harder to find than with others. Neptune is often strongly aspected in the charts of musicians, artists, sculptors, photographers, movie makers and other artistes of various shapes and sizes.

The neutral aspects of Neptune

Here is found the genuine sensitive, the person who wants nothing more than for their efforts than to be of benefit to those less fortunate than themselves. These people enjoy going to the movies and the theatre and don't normally go down the road of gratification, sensation or over stimulus. Neptune is most commonly experienced as the steadily increasing degree and desire for subtlety and aestheticism, it is where you come to appreciate the more refined sides of life and becomes steadily more gentle and compassionate as you age. You know that you are experiencing Neptune when you can look at your loved one through rose-coloured spectacles and consciously choose to see their good sides rather than the difficult ones, or when you see yourself winning the world cup for your country or in the latest blockbuster or romcom. It's where you can see yourself as the provider and generous one, or the dictatorial tyrant, but remember that all the world's a stage and all the people merely players. If the world around you is a movie, does that make you the casting director?

The difficult aspects to Neptune

When Neptune is in a bad way in your chart, you can never quite tell what type of subtle but undermining influence he can have. Neptune by his nature is nebulous and creates an energy of dissolution and uncertainty. It is where the escapism and avoidance of life can sometimes sap your energy to the point of exhaustion. Neptune can be where you allow yourself to be seduced or where you can choose to ignore the reality of the world instead favouring it as being the way you want it to be. Neptune is where you can put people on pedestals or see the world through rose-coloured spectacles. It can be where structures simple dissolve like sand and water through your fingers or it can be where you truly con yourself in ways that are at best gullible and at worst self-deceptive.

Neptune in a difficult light can be represented as muddled thinking and is sometimes associated with periods of depression. It can lead to fanciful notions and false projections and one of its worse qualities is that of allowing everything to impact all at once, creating a neurotic mess or puddle on the floor. Neptune is the prime escapist and fantasist, bringing a much greater sensitivity to things like narcotics, chemical drugs, alcohol and food additives as well as other people's dogma. A difficult Neptune can lead to the individual being easily swayed or led by others.

Neptune in aspect to Venus or Mars

Neptune's interaction with the sensual and sexual sides of life can be very vague, confusing and mysterious, as well as being visionary, enlightening and spiritual at the same time. Certainly it can be the symbolic representation of a number of different forms of neurosis, born seemingly of nothing but ungrounded worry but it also brings alongside this the faith and conviction needed to transcend the more negative habit pattering and conditioning of youth and instead emerge into a world of clarity, focus and unconditional love. There will be times with Neptune of 'falling' in love or of being seduced or enchanted, bewitched even, but alongside this there will always be the potential to find that level of beauty and empathy in your relationships with others that surpasses expectation.

There are three generalised types of Neptunian personality when it comes to the sexual and sensual side of life and these types are determined not only by Neptune's house position but also by its aspects to other points in your horoscope, particularly with Venus and Mars. The aspects between Neptune and other planets, particularly the Sun and the Moon, will dictate issues of identity, individuality and purpose and go beyond the area of sex and relationship but aspects of Neptune to Venus and Mars show the ways in which we as individuals respond to the intuitive, visionary and neurotic sides of our procreative nature.

Neptune in aspect to Venus

In many different schools of astrological thought, Neptune is seen as the higher octave of Venus. Venus represents what it is that we appreciate and enjoy in terms of physical comforts, warmth, company and wealth, whilst Neptune aspires to all that is beautiful, elegant, refined, sophisticated and aesthetic. When Venus and Neptune work well together it really can be beauty personified. There can be a charm and elegance that creates inspiration and all sorts of subtle nuances that give a frisson of love and all that goes with it. Even the healthy aspects from Venus to Neptune carry with them a health warning in that the contacts between these two sensual and artistic influences can be so strong that there can be a tendency to ignore the harsher realities of the world and instead bask in the surrealness of their own movie.

Neptune in difficult aspect to Venus can carry with it a kind of consumptive energy, where you can never be loved or appreciated enough and the true meaning of glamour (to enchant, to cast a glamour) can be demonstrated. It can be seen as relatively common in cases of addiction, whether to alcohol, drugs, tobacco or just addicted to the idea of being in love. This is not to ignore the positive side of this combination. When they work well together in the chart of someone who is not going to be swept away by their own charm, this aspect produces a high quality of artistic, musical or other forms of aesthetic response, often to a very high quality of degree. The greatest composers, film directors, actors/actresses and dancers are likely to have a powerful and healthy aspect between Neptune and Venus in their chart.

Neptune in aspect to Mars

The combination of Neptune and Mars can be quite an unholy one if certain observations are not acknowledged. Mars in its lower expression can be solely concerned with matters of the flesh and Neptune in a bad way can bring hedonism and escapism, so a combination of these two planets needs treating with a pair of tongs and fireproof gloves. Even the healthy combinations have a degree of simmering going on just underneath the surface, although the flowing aspects are more manageable than the challenging. In all mixes of these two horny planets there is a need for physical expression in a way that joins body and spirit and if you are single then regular visits to the local trance dance club are recommended. The difficult aspects can bring real confusion between what is dreamed fantasy and what can be creatively constructed from the imagination and there can be periodic losses of energy or vitality.

Here is found the sculptor, the architect, the mime artist, someone who uses the body and the imagination to create a work of art that espouses the creative side of your physicality. Here also is found the sexual hedonist with no boundaries and a propensity for viral or toxic infection, so attention to your physical bodily health is a must with these people. Perhaps the weirdest combination in the solar system, this mix needs to be given the freedom to develop its more independent side but at the same time to be mature enough to know when things are getting toxic and to set in place sensible firewalls against excess and indulgence.

Neptune sextile Venus or Mars

As mentioned before, a sextile is an aspect of opportunity. It blends the opportunistic with the hard working and blends the talent for artistic expression with the necessary energy and effort. It creates a warm and sensual receptiveness to the significant other in your life and individuals with this aspect in their chart tend to empathise and resonate with what is going on for their partner as much as if not more so than they resonate with what's going on for themselves.

With Venus, this is not to the point of transference or projection; instead this aspect brings a genuine amount of care and concern for their partner's well-being. This is the person who before luring and tempting you into the communal bed chamber will make sure that the pillows are fluffed up, that there are ample supplies of food and drink to hand and that all the little luxuries that make your love life more enjoyable are pre-thought of and to hand. Venus sextile Neptune knows exactly when to say enough and rarely, if ever, oversteps the mark. It is one of the most graceful of aspects and doesn't like to find itself in situations of coarseness or gross behaviour. This is the person who will enjoy a string quartet followed by a long and pleasurable meal with champagne before going to bed with partner and relaxing into a bout of sensual, gentle and mutually warm pleasure, as opposed to a rock concert, beer and chips and 'wham bam thank you ma'am' which is so unsophisticated, so basic, so 'Mars, dahling…'

Whereas Mars sextile Neptune has a much more physical and adventurous side to it, with an innate understanding of the blend of your emotional and physical urges, resulting in a creative talent being released much of the time. The opportunity to be physically creative generally gives a good constitution and a healthy attitude towards sex with an open and experimental attitude. Music helps you 'get into the rhythm', whether that rhythm is on the dance floor, in the bedroom or in the workplace. Certainly, dance, yoga, drama, tai chi, qi gong, sex, pilates or any other form of physical movement that you can put your passion into is recommended. There is the energy available to put into your partner when they are low without keeping score and there is a generally relaxed attitude towards your partner and your life with them. The straightforward approach works in almost all cases.

Neptune trine Venus or Mars

Whilst the keyword for a sextile is opportunity, the keyword for a trine is talent and a trine between Venus or Mars and Neptune is perhaps the nicest aspect of all for talent in the performing or artistic world as it brings in and emphasises the interplay between the physically demonstrative, the emotionally evocative and the artistically creative as well as essences of both the intuitive and the spiritual.

The grace and elegance that Venus often demonstrates works exceptionally well with Neptune's more refined and aesthetic nature. These are the people who are comfortable in a number of different artistic environments, although there is a distinct dislike of the coarse, loud, gross and unsubtle. There will be a natural receptivity to all types of artistic phenomena, especially the more passive forms such as going to the movies, theatre or dance or any other type of observational art form that brings an element of appreciation and pleasure into the senses. In the bedroom these are very much the sensual and delicate lovers, who like to explore every nook and cranny of their partner's body in order to learn how to bring them the greatest sensual pleasure.

These people know that the best way to show love doesn't automatically involve sex as much as it involves stroking, tickling, laughing and gently making both partners feel totally at ease with each other. These are the people who more than any others know the difference between being in love and falling in love and who can taste the temptation without being overly seduced or enchanted by what can be mere fantasy. It suggests a healthy and strong combination of dreamy romanticism with sensible and well-balanced attitudes towards love, sex and relationships.

The trine between Mars and Neptune brings an integration of action and dreams. This combination somehow manages to surf the edges and get out of harm's way without even realising it. It brings a subtle capacity for action, not so much pronounced as quieter, behind the scenes but just as effective. There exists the ability to spot someone who is not telling the truth the second that they open their mouth and the more this ability is trusted the stronger it gets, bringing a healthy blend of physical energy and psychic perception ensuring that the wool doesn't get pulled over your eyes. A trine suggests a harmonic blending of similar energies and when Mars and Neptune combine gracefully the artisticness of physicality is stressed, hence this aspect being prominent in the lives of those who become actors, mime artists or other forms of performer or public entertainer in the physical world.

Neptune square Venus or Mars

A square is a dynamic aspect that links together two energies that have nothing in common, creating a pattern of obstruction, challenge and friction. However, standing resolute is not Neptune's way. In a square pattern his method of behaviour is that of slow decay, crumbling things from the edges and bringing a degree of dissolving into your life. When this square of Neptune is to Venus and/or Mars, then the whole issue of relationship and the evolution of it comes under the ever-changing spotlight. It is true that difficult aspects to Neptune can bring a greater preponderance of the deceptive into your relationship patterns but whether that is to you or from you, whether it is intentional or unmeant, or whether or not you connive in your own deception all depends on the sign and house that the aspect falls in as much as the aspect itself.

With Venus square Neptune, your sense of self-worth and self-evaluation can be steadily dissolved to the point where you can become permanently disappointed in the types of relationship that you attract. Self-deception is just as likely, if not more so, than deception by others. Instead, the person with the Venus/Neptune square will give and give in the hope that they will be appreciated whilst at the same time secretly hoping for a happy end to the fairy story, that their partner will 'come true'. There can be a sense of bottomless love, in that the individual with this position can never really be loved enough no matter how much comes their way.

These people yearn for the unachievable and the impossible, with a passion that can border on the pathological. Once the individual with the Venus/Neptune square finds themselves becoming the doormat or self-sacrificing, then co-dependency or even servitude can become the norm. There can be an element of self-neglect when it comes to the financial side of life but predominantly this aspect focuses on the bed chamber and the desire for the fantasy and dream world that promises so much safety and security but normally delivers little except instability until you learn the wisdom of not always going to extremes and instead finding pleasure in the middle ground.

Mars squaring Neptune is less self-reflective and more self-projective. It is where the individual can go through sudden periods of weariness, of lack of libido and of physical exhaustion. Here also is found the shamanistic practitioner who works the fringes, sieves the opportunities and embraces the slightly weird and off beam. Mars square Neptune can be the ultimate hedonist, anxious to sample everything at least once and there can be a superficial attitude to relationship as a result. Even those with the perfect relationship will still look at other people in the street and wonder. It is the 'what if?' that powers the creative imagination that this aspect releases but that effect can be brief, leading to sudden infatuations and momentary fascination, even brief fixation. Neptune will always feel that Mars is too fast and hot so will drown him out and try and dampen his ardour; whereas Mars will see Neptune as the sticky bubble-gum that he is trying to pull himself from, needing occasional lasers of spontaneity to make it happen.

Neptune opposite Venus or Mars

An opposition from Neptune always carries with it an element of fascination, of entrancement, mystery and seduction and when this opposition is to Venus or Mars, the guessing games of love and life come strongly into the equation. "What does he mean by that?" "What is she thinking?" "Are those real signals or am I just making them up?" The potential for projection, for seeing someone as being the way that you want them to be as opposed to accepting them as the way they are is strong. You can end up putting other people on pedestals, which makes them both unobtainable and a lot easier to tumble.

Neptune is always associated with the nebulous and the invisible and the opposition from Neptune to Venus or Mars has been linked with a more open and experimental approach to sex. It should be noted that Neptune in invisible mode is often the bearer of bad or confusing news and in one of his guises he is the ruler of toxins and forms of poison that can insidiously invade, so along with an open approach to sensuality and sexuality there also needs to be a grounded and common sensical approach to health issues, particularly concerning virals. These aspects will take you to heaven and they will take you to hell, sometimes simultaneously, they are the mark of the experiential, whether through addiction, hedonism or devotion.

Neptune opposite Venus

More than any other aspect in the zodiac, Venus opposite Neptune produces the fantasy, the projection and often the disappointment that comes when the image slips and reality is exposed. Yet there is always the boundless love needed to carry on and despite these people's tendencies to become easily drained by others, somehow they keep on giving. In time the wise ones realise that the more you give, the more you have got to give, energy flows and the batteries stay charged whereas those who constantly pine and dream of what might be instead of making what they have the best often end up unfulfilled. There is the need for a reality check every so often, which is where close friends with no agenda come in useful. Otherwise you may find yourself easily conned, duped, seduced or gullible.

You are who you are, warts and all and so is everyone else. Once that basic self-acceptance is made, you become much better relationship material. There will always be the need for enchantment, romance and fascination so make sure that your relationships are never too staid, that there will always be room for a little romance as much as anything else. If you have this aspect in your chart you are going to want a partner that enjoys going to the movies and theatre, travelling to exotic and romantic or even idyllic locations and who is as sensual and receptive as you are but without become co-dependent or needful on each other or deliberately clouding issues so that you don't have to deal with them.

With Venus opposite Neptune you can be the femme fatale, the mystery woman or for that matter the Lothario leaping from the balcony with a rose between his teeth. It doesn't really matter what role you play in the bedroom as long as you realise that much of the time you are playing that role and you are not letting yourself slip into the role of victim too much. You don't care what your prospective partner looks like as long as they have got some imagination. As a general rule of thumb, bedroom antics and alcohol are an unholy mix as it lowers already fragile boundaries and confuses the perception. However, a tropical island, pink champagne, exquisite food and the perfect partner alongside you in that type of environment means that perception can afford to be a bit fuzzy and the wishful fantasy can be lived, if only for a brief time.

Under the bedcovers these are the people who will play charades, daring you to uncover them or to find out who they are pretending to be. The safest way to their heart is with gentle and kind persistence, flowers, charm, sophistication, chocolate, subtlety, compassion and a love of the higher forms of sensuality. Remember that more than any other aspect, Venus opposite Neptune is par excellence for falling in love as opposed to being in love and needs constant reality checks to ensure that at least one foot is on the ground at all times.

Neptune opposite Mars

Without a doubt one of the strangest aspects in astrology, when it comes to the sexual side of life this aspect seems to have a life of its own. The physical and demonstrative side of Mars in opposition to the vague and nebulous qualities of Neptune creates a great deal of huffing and puffing but often this aspect runs out of steam before it gets to the final lap. Yet when used in a way that is projective without being confrontational or overly assertive, the Mars energy can be infused with the more refined qualities of Neptune, giving a masterful degree of physical power. This can be through dance, martial arts or another form of physical practice that has an element of the mysterious and esoteric about it but this can also be seen in the worst cases of self-indulgence, addiction and wilful ignorance. It can be the warrior priest, or the hopeless drunk or junkie.

More than any other position, Mars opposite Neptune knows that the world is not always the way it seems to be and that as long as you are able to maintain clear distinctions within yourself about the difference between fantasy and imagination (one stays in the head, the other can be created) you can surf the edges and make the world the way you want it to be, as long as you are maintaining your conscience and integrity. This aspect has a habit of sabotaging those people with it who act in a behind the scenes or duplicit manner, often through either self-guilt or self-doubt, resulting in a kind of entropy or apathy where despite the best intentions, little if anything ever really gets done.

If you are partnered with one of these active dreamers, your sex life is going to be anything but quiet. Here is the all-conquering hero coming to claim their rightful partner, or alternatively the helpless victim at the mercy of the cruel master or mistress. They love role playing and with this type of partner you can be sure that your sex life won't be mundane. At the very least there will be a great deal of tickling but this aspect actively encourages those with it to experiment in ways that aren't necessarily to all tastes, so they have to be mature and responsible enough to remember that all interplay has to be consensual lest it become unhealthy. It creates a fertile and dynamic highly charged drive that sometimes just fizzles out prematurely but if managed responsibly and creatively it gives the potential for the sexual experience to be the vehicle for both partners to attain a higher frequency of both sensual and spiritual experience.

Neptune conjunct Venus

Venus and Neptune respond to each other in a similar way to Mars and Pluto in that one is the lower, more physical and material manifestation whilst the other is the higher, aesthetic and more subtle way of seeing things. Whilst Venus' principle role is that of value and worth mixed with appreciation and pleasure, Neptune tends to operate more on the fringes bringing a tinge of variation and enchantment into the equation. Venus conjunct Neptune brings a degree of beauty, unconditional love and gentility into your life but the difficult part of this is knowing what is real and what is imaginary or fantasy. Both of these planets yearn for the unreachable in terms of soul partner, life mate etc. and this can and often does result in the phenomena of falling in love instead of being in love, inevitably resulting in disappointment when the partner falls from the pedestal that Venus/Neptune puts them on.

For those who use this energy outside of personal relationship patterns, this combination is perhaps the best of all for those artists who respond to a different vibration than the rest of us, bringing out the angelic painter, the euphoric musician/composer or the envisioned sculptor. On the one hand this position can be the artist who can make something tangible out of the creative imagination whilst on the other it is the hopeless fantasist who has little touch with reality, often leading to either neurosis, addiction of some type or complete withdrawal from the world into a kind of hermit-like existence.

Taken in the context of the more personal and intimate side of love, Venus and Neptune together can bring a wide variety of potential into the bedroom. More often than not, the feminine and receptive nature of these two planetary energies brings a more passive attitude which can sometimes be mistaken for submissiveness. These are the water bed specialists who enjoy the constant wave motion and who can dance to a higher rhythm with their partner. These people love being in love and will often enjoy their sex life with their eyes closed, preferring not to be distracted by the visual. The sensible ones with this position really don't care what you look like, they appreciate you for how you make them feel. These are the real sensation junkies and they are likely to be really turned off by the more assertive and dynamic attitudes shown by some towards sex. They want to be stroked and gently massaged as they are made love to, preferably with the sound of the waves in the background and a cooled glass of wine within reach. Did I mention the strawberries or the chocolate?

At the same time, they can become hopelessly addicted to their partners, willing to do anything or be anyone just so long as they are not feeling left or abandoned. In most cases, it is inevitable that at some time during their sexual experimentation, cream cakes will enter into the equation. Either that or some other form of gooey, honey-like slithery lubricant that can be licked or showered off. There can be an almost pathological need to be loved which invariably leads to some type of surrender of autonomy but the other side of the same coin is that of the person who really does understand the principle of unconditional love, creating a degree of beauty around them through this process that nobody in their right mind would ever want to leave. When they finally realise that their external personal and intimate relationship patterns are a mirror-like reflection of the relationship that they have with themselves, they grow into a fully mature and loving individual with lots to give and little expected back.

Neptune conjunct Mars

Mars is the capacity for being assertive and projective, hopefully without being aggressive or confrontational. It is how you use your physical energy, whether that manifests as walking the dog, down the gym, digging the garden or in the bedroom. Neptune is the more nebulous, vague, aesthetic and brings the artistic and the spiritual into the equation. When these two planets are in the same place in a person's chart there will always be an active imagination to the point where occasionally these people need to be reminded that whilst the imagination can be actively created, the fantasy stays firmly between the ears. When this combination manifests itself in a challenging way there can be a degree of hedonism that knows no boundaries, often resulting in the more invisible physical problems such as virus, energy depletion and toxin.

When manifested positively, the blend of physicality and spirituality can bring the highest form of projective art such as sculpture, drama and particularly dance. Dance, especially euphoric, trance-like dance breaks down normal barriers of individuality and when on the dance floor it is easy to just 'go with the flow' with the result that you can dance for hours without thinking, thus giving both the body and soul a good workout and a conjoining of energies within a synergetic community around you. Mars conjunct Neptune can be found in the charts of film makers, sculptors, photographers and other forms of artist that uses the physical contours of the body as an artistic prop.

At the same time, a phenomenon commonly associated with this position is sudden and unexplainable loss of physical energy, often only for a few minutes or hours at a time with no sign of illness, just sudden weariness. The sensible person with this aspect is able to recognise this and knows when to stop and allow the body to recharge, often done best in a bath or sauna, or at least get a few minutes alone to discharge and recharge.

As far as the physical and sexual side of Neptune conjunct Mars goes, here is the land of the truly weird and wonderful. Every time the person with this aspect tries to establish boundaries, ethics or codes of behaviour in their personal and intimate lifestyle, something changes that dissolves those boundaries. There can be no consistency with this position but there can be a great deal of variation, which of course can significantly affect the levels of pleasure that are mutually experienced.

This is the person who will lightly tie you down and eat fresh strawberries and cream off of your body and then on the next day ask you to whip them with wet celery. There can be a degree of willing powerlessness and powerfulness with this position and they should ensure that domination or subjugation issues do not go to extremes and that all interaction is consensual, lest they lose sight of their boundaries and become a slave to their lower base desires. Variation in their love making positions, settings and environments is always important to them; they thrive on the atmosphere created by different environments, particularly if the environment in question is outdoors or in some other form of exposed position.

Whilst they would be mortified to be caught doing anything even remotely kinky, there is still the thrill of taking risks, often exemplified by al fresco lovemaking whether in the fields, forests or in the sea (recommended!). Mars/Neptune conjunctions can take you to heaven or hell in terms of sensation and only the wise ones with this position who know when to stop within self-imposed boundaries are really able to take best advantage of this hot and cold aspect.

13

Pluto

Death, rebirth and transformation

Pluto is perhaps the most misunderstood of the planets, shrouded in darkness and almost cursed by its mythology. Pluto has represented all that is hidden and secret and only in the twenty-first century is a new approach to Pluto finally surfacing out of its Hadean depths. Pluto deals with the really difficult stuff. Quite how it works is anyone's guess because as the scientists will clearly say how can a lump of rock smaller than our Moon and over four billion miles away have such an effect? Astrologically there is clear evidence as to its effects and despite astronomical scientists' recent attempts to downgrade Pluto's status from being a planet to being a dwarf planet, its effects are increasingly becoming apparent in a number of ways.

The down side of Pluto is its capacity for obsession and compulsion, crisis and trauma, intensity and extremes. Already it should be clear that astrologically Pluto is no lightweight. It brings an irrational attitude towards attaining your goals no matter what the cost and can be apparently ruthless and unstoppable in its desire to have its own way. During Plutonian times in your life this can bring people into your journey that feel threatened by your actions and may try to stop you in ways that can incur typical Plutonian courses of action, such as jealousy, power struggles, behind the scenes manipulation of various types (mental, verbal, emotional and sexual), hidden agendas or even outright confrontation and aggression.

Of course, much of this can be seen as other people being scared of losing you so they will try and stop you in ways that can be clearly seen as based on fear of loss as opposed to outright opposition but every so often with Pluto, there is the need to watch your back. Pluto is Hades in other language, the lord of the underworld and the secret holder of all of our fears, phobias and paranoias but he is quite willing to let them out into the light at the appropriate time. He takes us down into what some call our own internal psychological roots and foundations and ensures that we get to the bottom of things no matter what the cost.

The neutral side of Pluto is shown in its capacity for decision and action regardless of outcome. Pluto will destroy, totally. It will eliminate and purify, detox and cleanse in a way that is clinically self-purging and that gets to the bottom of every part of everything, scouring all the secret little holes so that there is no negativity left. Periodically people go through times of detox, whether physical, mental, emotional or spiritual or a combination of them all, on their pathway to spiritual regeneration. Pluto is the planet of death and rebirth and it works on the principle that the old must die before the new is born.

People with powerful positions of Pluto in their chart go through huge challenges in life where periodically they attempt to almost destroy themselves in some purgative urge to remould, remake and renew at a fresher and more evolved level. Here Pluto's willingness to recycle and transform matter into something more refined and cleaner becomes clearer. Through the elimination of waste and the purification and cleansing of remaining residue Pluto symbolically facilitates the ongoing process of transformation into something higher and less easily manipulated.

The positive side of Pluto, when it finally emerges out of its cavernous depths, is that of regeneration, transformation and rebirth at the highest of order. It represents the time of the potential for the individual to rise to their most psychologically mature and emotionally invulnerable. Pluto is sometimes seen when young as the caterpillar metamorphosing into the butterfly, refining itself into a higher state of consciousness and gaining a broader, more multi-dimensional perspective. As one approaches and lives through middle ages Pluto's analogical figure becomes the snake shedding its skin and emerging more streamlined and less burdened, more focussed and directed and capable of entering and leaving situations with more effectiveness and efficiency.

For those people willing to undergo Pluto's psychological examinations and challenges knowing their fear and with nothing to hide, its highest manifestation is that of the phoenix rising, pure and regenerated from the ashes of the old and dead. Death and rebirth in a constant cycle of transformation and regeneration is the higher meaning of Pluto for many. It represents our deepest fears and our highest aspirations and our constant willingness or refusal to deal with the darker sides of our nature, both collectively and individually.

Pluto through the houses

Later on there will be specific references to the meanings of the different aspects between Venus and Mars with Pluto for both the positive and challenging but the following list of attributes and difficulties of Pluto in each house sets the background for internal and external psychological development through the areas of sex and relationship and hopefully gives a guide on how to manage this most difficult of planets in ways that are transparent and above board, thus attracting only positive transformation and no opposition.

Pluto in the first house

Here in the area of identity Pluto insists that the relationship you have with yourself must first of all be transformed before any significant quality can come into any of your relationships with other. There will be a degree of intensity in all of your personal interactions and some may find you a little compulsive or intimidating. Indeed, if you find yourself completely a fish out of water you may become angry at yourself for no apparent reason. Good responses to people's nosy questions are, 'Why do you want to know?" You can be protective of your personal romantic interests but at the same time very good at ferreting out other people's secrets.

Pluto here brings a thirst for direct experience and the desire for self-sufficiency with the idea of being dependent on others in some way disempowering. There can be a fear of being overpowered and yet at the same time a secret attraction to the same thing leading to an element of the 'I dare you to suss me out' persona, guaranteed to attract both the interesting and also the challenging. Periods of self-doubt and identity crisis are seen as the precursor to elevating yourself into a higher relationship dynamic but in the background there is always going to be the awareness that because of your powerful drive towards transformation and regeneration you will inevitably burn out those more sensitive souls and that you can only comfortably co-exist with those who are also on a path of self-transformation. Consequently, bedroom activity for people with Pluto in the first house can go through prolonged periods of abstinence followed by periods of real gluttony but the essence here is on the one hand filling and charging your batteries but on the other hand also putting energy into others so that in the future you won't be so alone. There will come in relationships times when you will go through powerful subconscious drives that seem beyond your ability to control and where your drive for personal power can be seen as overly strong and not well managed, so keep things clean and transparent to avoid accusations of acting in devious or underhand ways. Others will see you as mysterious, a bit obsessive and occasionally something of a loner but better that than forming associations with inappropriate people or people who are not transparent in their actions towards you. Strive towards a simple and clean lifestyle and you will attract similar people into your life.

Pluto in the second house

Your values and sense of priorities in relationships are at question here as increasingly other people in your one-to-one relationships make you question what it is that you really want from them. With Pluto in the house of possessions and worth opportunities for transforming yourself through the use of material resources and financial power will occur at intervals in your life. If these are incorporated into ways of working with your significant other then a synergetic approach to resources can bring not only a transformation of personal relationship and all that goes with it but also a mutual approach to the outside world that is relationship transforming. Any area of working with other that incorporates ideas such as converting raw materials into effective tools, combating pollution, rubbish recycling, professions delving into psychological motives and mutual detective work of all kinds will work out fine.

Watch out for the more base types of people or becoming involved in any form of criminal activity because this lowers your vibe and will almost certainly lead to conflict with authorities at some stage. Greed and overly materialistic attitudes can be a danger and this can bring sudden wealth but also the unexpected losses that invariably follow. There is a need for a basic self-discipline with regard to material possessions and the lower evolved people with this position count their partners as possessions.

They like to feel that they have control of bedroom activities by rationing their love, the food, the power, the cash etc. It just gives them the feeling of control that they so badly crave. They don't like to think of themselves as alone so they will resort to any means necessary to try and persuade people to be or stay with them, some of which may seem a little tenuous or even unethical but these people do attach sentimental value to their past and sometimes have difficulty recognising that over a period of time, other people change. The inverse side of this position is that whilst they can sometimes collect people almost like mementos, others who try and collect them or take things from them can really arouse their anger.

Pluto in the second house brings a sense of belonging, a sense of ownership and value that doesn't like to be challenged because challenge threatens long-term stability, something precious to these perhaps quite insecure people. Cuddle them loads, tell them that you want them for who they are and reassure them that they are the most important thing to you and you will have a devoted slave in the bedroom and a contented equal in other areas. Just don't remind them of their lowly position because then their stubborn streak becomes unmanageable. At the end of the day people with this position attract others towards them who help them develop a good sense of worth.

Pluto in the third house

Don't let your relationships become brother/sister-like as this can create an overly versatile communication dynamic that can evolve into something slightly bitter or resentful, similar in ways to unfulfilled promises. You may find difficulty in learning to trust others at the one-to-one level, something that only changes with both time and prolonged exposure to honest and trustworthy people. There will always be a quest for hidden meanings until you learn to take people at face value regardless of what your mind is saying.

The natural inquisitiveness that this position generates, both of yourself and of others, leads to a very powerful concentration which when allowed to run unchecked can descend into mental turmoil.

Don't disregard the mind but store it for later and in the meantime take people as you find them unless proven otherwise. You can be persuasive and decisive with others at times to the point of abruptness whilst at other times you can be almost indecisive and conciliatory. There is a tendency over time to learn through observation rather than by asking specific questions. When young there is the desire for self-education and direct experience as opposed to listening to the advice of others or finding out from text books, which kind of makes it hard to settle down into long-term relationships unless you are partnered with an intellectual equal who shares your level of passion or intensity. When older, Pluto grabs this mobile and intellectual energy and often manifests itself as specialised teaching skills.

There can be the tendency for Pluto in the third house people to be overly verbose on the one hand and superficial on the other making it very difficult to pin yourself down in terms of specific attitude or opinion, probably caused by a deep-rooted fear of letting others know too much about you. With this position opportunities for adapting, transforming or regenerating yourself come through other people's communication initiatives and through understanding and working with their ideas you can form very deep insights on life, death and the transformative process that lies between. Your relationships should provide you with the bridge to reform and improve your ability to communicate and to write or express the issues of the day in a way that becomes increasingly profound with age and experience, although on the negative side there can be a tendency to occasional morbidity with periods of dwelling, depression or preoccupation with the deeper sides of life. You need to be partnered with someone who ascribes to the levels of depth that you sometimes go to but who also can bring you out of yourself through banter and superficial silliness and occasional periods of either deliberate silences or attempts at mime, so that you don't become so totally dependent on the vocal side of life.

Pluto in the fourth house

There will always be the potential here for unresolved issues to do with parents influencing your adult relationship patterning, although this isn't automatically the case. Don't expect your relationships to be like your parents were because that's a recipe for disaster. It may have been that you feel insecure in some shape or form about your childhood, which is all well and good because many people do. However, it would be inappropriate for you to allow these experiences to affect your adult relationship life because to do so would bring parent-child roles into the relationship dynamic, creating an energy perhaps not applicable for happy one-to-one relationships based on teamwork and healthy interplay. It's really important that you don't draw on your past for guidelines on how to deal with current day relationships, regardless of whether that past is based on pride, guilt or somewhere in between. It's just as important, if not more so, that you deal with each emerging situation on its own merits because the capacity for behaving in entrenched reactive patterns here is the strongest that there is.

More than almost any other position you need to adapt to the current times regularly to avoid becoming caught in the past and its own form of almost compulsive obsession, which in truth is nothing to do with you but is probably just the projection of a parent who wanted you to be what they could have been if they had taken their chances.

The risk with this position is that of a tendency to dominate and coerce others at the one-to-one level which could alienate them against you and create a power struggle within the boundaries of the family structure. Any old influence that belongs in the past needs to be released otherwise there can always be either an Oedipal or Electra complex present which plays havoc with same age personal relationship patterns. There may be some mystery or secret relating to home activities and this is strictly confined to the family circle. If so, this needs to be brought out and eliminated so that quality relationships can prosper and grow without being influenced in a slightly grimy way by the indiscretions of the past. Be the family rebel who voices all the old secrets! No one will mess with you then...

The greatest potential here is that of transforming your life into one where you act as the parent, grandparent, protector and nurturer without interfering with other people's free will or personal choice, whilst the danger is expecting others to be the way you want them to be without allowing them either the room to grow or the freedom of choice. Someone with Pluto in the fourth house needs the type of partner who will be not only a confidante but also a therapist on the quiet especially in the bedroom. Deeply emotive and passionate but scared to show it, these souls need warmth and reassurance in order to let their true beauty show. They will transform the ways in which you live and help you have a much better all-round quality of life, just don't let them completely take over.

Pluto in the fifth house

Do you want to be the world's greatest lover, with the power to make people fall in love with you? You can if you wish but you will pay... Pluto here makes you look at your own ideas of beauty and asks you what it is that has worth. Your creative impulse is strong and when it comes to the art of being procreative then you will find that your relationships with both your lovers and your children teach you much about human dynamics. When young, there can be an arrogance and sense of overly stretched pride in yourself that invariably leads to becoming alone and friendless at various times in your life, which then will lead to an all or nothing approach to life and love. This is probably caused by feelings of being misunderstood by at least one of their parents. There can be the tendency for people with Pluto in the fifth house to be overly protective or else to attract people toward them who seek to have such a controlling influence in their life that it borders on the manipulative, so caution is advised. It is OK being in love, it's the falling in love that brings the problems and the intensity you bring to your bedroom affairs will be rarely superficial or light hearted.

There will always be the deep-rooted desire to transform all of your love-based experiences into something higher but one person's salvation is another's damnation and sometimes you just have to let others be the way that they are and get used to it, at least in the bedroom. Either that or leave so this is the put up, tolerate, or shut up position at certain times. Certainly there will be both the potential and the desire to transform lower sexual energy into something more creative and innovative and there exists the opportunity to really transform sexual energy. Pluto in the fifth house will always have a taste for the more unusual and esoteric and sex will go through real periods of emphasis in that at times you may find yourself attracted to secret or unconventional relationships or at least play that role in your existing relationship. Any type of underhand financial speculation is really not advised, on the grounds that just because you think that you are lucky doesn't mean that you are. The best thing about this position is its willingness to have fun with its significant other and the worst thing is their tendency to try and gain control of relationships through childlike tantrums or similar behaviour patterns.

Pluto in the sixth house

With Pluto here you may find yourself feeling almost obsessively compelled to explore areas of pain and purity in your life, it is as though if it is not hurting then it's not working. The worst extremists and the cleanest and purest of souls both live here so be warned that this is not an area for the fainthearted. With this position opportunities for transforming or regenerating yourself are likely to come through professional career or work environment but in this area as well as your one-to-one relationships it is important that you remember to make allowances for others, because no one will quite match up to your exacting standards.

If you focus too much on work you may find yourself becoming increasingly alienated from partner or family so obviously a good balance is needed here and the most obvious way of telling whether or not this is happening is by looking at your diet and nutrition. Other people may see you as a bit of a health nut on the side but a correct diet, proper exercise and a positive mental attitude will dramatically enhance your life and a willingness to work with others in the name of service or duty will make you wildly popular. Whilst your work is important and necessary in order to keep your vital juices flowing, you shouldn't let this become too obsessive because if you do it will be at the expense of a number of your close relationships.

Don't let work and family issues overlap or else there can be criticism from both areas that will only undermine your confidence and once again push you into isolation. As far as the bedroom goes there can be a fixation with the extremities of the body. Here is found the finger and toe-sucker. These are the people who live to get all dirty during sex, whether that dirt is good old-fashioned mud, or honey, or chocolate or anything that helps the slithering process. Of course, a nearby shower is absolutely necessary. In fact, this somewhat repressed position of Pluto has it in itself to be the most disgusting and depraved of sexual animals but if they are not careful, they price both themselves and all others out of the market. Never going to be good enough, you have to remind yourself that you are always getting better but you are never going to be as perfect as you can dream. Neither is anyone else in your life ever going to be good enough but as long as they are doing their best then that has to be OK or else you run the risk of being seen as a hard taskmaster and not given to flexibility, hardly the best recommendation for quality relationship. Lighten up and go easy on yourself, you are still as good as you can be and that'll do, at least for the ongoing moment.

Pluto in the seventh house

It is through your interactions with other at the one-to-one level that the most meaningful but also the most personal transformations will occur because sometimes other people's needs do take precedence and that's what teamwork is all about. Sweet surrender and all that… With Pluto here the normal power struggles in relationship patterns are not so much common as strong and where they exist they can be played out in a number of different ways. You may find out that without meaning to you apparently bring out the worst in others simply by giving them the space and time to fully express themselves, even to extremes, so in a kind of weird way if others let off steam, or worse at you, it's because they trust you enough to do so, which is a backhanded compliment if ever there was one.

Alternatively, you may find yourself compulsively attracted to people in the world who want you to be a powerful and dominant figure in their life, or they may try and be that figure to you, either knowingly or unconsciously to the point of obsession. There can be a quality of absorption either towards or from you to be aware of and even manipulation if there is any sign of fear, loss or rejection on your part. It's important to realise here that it takes two to tango and there is never just one perpetrator and one victim, that both partners take equal responsibility for the sanctity of the relationship. If you are seeing something that you don't like in your partner you have to first of all know it in yourself in order to recognise it in them, so make sure that you don't project loss or betrayal of any type onto your significant other because that's the easiest way to ensure that the relationship will collapse into mutual recrimination.

With Pluto in the seventh house of interactive partnerships opportunities for transforming or regenerating yourself are likely to come through close personal relationships, social or business partnerships, often in various different combinations at the same time and even with the same person. General well-being and personal success are deemed as dependant on making successes of your most intimate and fulfilling relationships and success in your relationships depends on how responsible you are in your dealings with others. There is a need to establish clear and specific boundaries between your personal and your professional life and if they overlap there may be not only confusion but also added stress in both areas, leading to both potentially collapsing. Know when to work and when and with whom to play and keep the distinctions clear without letting other people muddy the water, either knowingly or otherwise, otherwise you will end up either kissing the boss or else patronising the partner, neither of which will endear you to others.

The core root of the seventh house position is your own willingness to see your one-to-one relationship patterns as a reflection in the outside world of the relationship you have with yourself and vice versa. The outer world and your interactions with the people in it at any given time mirror your internal status.

Pluto in the eighth house

Nowhere near as scary as its reputation but still a heavyweight character when dealing with the depth orientated sides of love and relationship, this is a position that inspires both respect and awe in equal measures. The problem will be if you are not strong enough within yourself to know when to stop and voluntarily allow the brakes to go on, as opposed to having them externally forced upon you. Sometimes you are like a dog with a bone not knowing how or when to back off and this can seriously scare people so know when to stop or run the risk of a degree of social exclusion.

There is an interest in the metaphysical ways of seeing the world and often a powerful intuition that goes with that interest. If you are able to come across as someone comfortable within their own power structures and in control of themselves and their environment, then you will command both respect and acknowledgement as someone influential and inspirational. Comfortable enough in the dark, it's the shades of grey that this position has the most difficulty with. With Pluto in the eighth house opportunities for transforming or regenerating self will come through a strong interest in occult studies or through other forms of metaphysical work and you will find yourself attracted to those types of people who also seek to probe the mysteries of life, death, sex and power.

Obviously there is nothing too lightweight with this position. There will be a natural tendency to seek out all that is hidden or taboo and relationship is the obvious playground for this type of exploration to the point that you can scare others off with your intensity and capacity for going to extremes, so remember when to lighten up and smell the coffee otherwise you will find yourself in an increasingly small world of one.

Almost inevitably sexual relationships will be the biggest challenge and mystery of all, with an almost morbid fascination for intimacy and depth as well as a potentially deep-rooted fear of it and you will find that over your life this will bring a number of deep and intense sexual encounters, some very fulfilling and others equally as wounding. There can be a tendency with Pluto in the eighth house to seek out people as borderline compulsive as yourself, because only by being in that degree of cutting edginess do you feel at your most effective and the only people you can truly be with are those who epitomise and relate to this degree of power.

Don't let yourself become too obsessed with issues of depth, control, dominance or submission because those deep pools can be extremely seductive and difficult to get out of once properly immersed. There is the need to remember to take yourself and partner to the funfair to have fun. It helps to regularly look at and review both your and your partner's attitudes towards power and the sharing of it as well as other forms of resource because without this regular re-evaluation there can be occasional power struggles, especially with money and financial upheavals that may periodically occur. There will always be issues of control here, it's just a question of whether those control issues are managed with openness and honesty or with fear and an unwillingness to face up to some of the realities of life.

Pluto in the ninth house

Over the course of a lifetime this position represents a transformation of beliefs and personal ethics in a way that brings an ever-simpler lifestyle and woe betide anyone who tries to bring complications into your life. You will find that when younger you may become extremely attached to your opinions and belief systems. Because of this you may find yourself commonly in the position of having to defend your opinions and actions unless you are careful. As you age so your needs become simpler and you value people in your life for their clarity and their ability to sail through life without too much sticking to them.

This position can bring strong potential for self-belief but also narrow-mindedness and a resistance to other people's ideas, often because you have done your research well and won't stand for any argument. Differences of opinion need to be tolerated otherwise you can be obsessed with 'converting' others to your beliefs and there almost certainly will be suspicions of new ideas until you have given them deeper thought, with a major disdain for blind followers of belief systems.

There is likely to be a deep running need for adventure and ideally they like their partners to be open to new and exciting things. There is a deep-rooted fear of mundanity and boredom, although in the bedroom these are the people who are likely to stop right in the middle of a hot and steamy encounter to say "Yes but what exactly do you mean by that?" and completely lose the moment.

At the end of the day you learn best by direct experience whether that is in the bedroom or by travelling and some of your most intense and life-changing unusual experiences may come through travel or in connection with other cultures. With Pluto in the ninth house of philosophy there can be opportunities for transforming or regenerating yourself through some type of recognition in some field of higher learning or other form of metaphysical or even religious study when older or more experienced. As you age so you are likely to be drawn to emotional and ancient religious sites and undergo the experience of other cultures and this is certainly best enjoyed in the company of significant other, on the grounds that sometimes two and two do make five especially where there is mutual learning to be shared. Certainly, the idea of foreign travel may feature strongly in your quest for profound knowledge although the tendency towards fanaticism or extremism of belief should be avoided.

Pluto in the tenth house

Are you really content to go it alone in the outside world, trusting no one and empowering only yourself? You may well be very successful but you won't necessarily be happy. Childhood impressions that last until adulthood can warp your interpretation of others' actions. You may find that others see you as ruthlessly ambitious, although this admittedly is an extreme but there can be a compulsive quality to the way you chase life goals, which will win both staunch admirers and vigorous opposition. Perhaps there is a previously unacknowledged place in your make up for a degree of both diplomacy and patience. Be sure that selfish and single-minded drives to success at the expense of other or others will fail. Change begins when you first feel the movement beyond basic ambition towards something more or better. As you deal with transformation of both self and your position in the world, so the potential for this career powered drive to disseminate into other areas of your life gets stronger but with Pluto in your tenth house, achieving a sense of power can definitely be among your ambitions.

If you decide not to follow a career path you can still be a powerful force for transformation in both relationship and family and will play an increasingly influential role as you mature. Before you can achieve the success you desire you may have to address old guilt or shame patterns which have their origins in childhood and the wise amongst you will allow your partner to lead in the bedroom, giving you the opportunity to surrender to a mild degree and let someone else take the responsibility and authority decisions for once.

There can be a radical side to your nature that has an almost dramatic urge to transform society and if you can do this with your personal partner alongside you then so much the better. You could be either a destructive or powerful force for healing and positive change in the world. With this position sometimes career can take precedence over relationship, in that relationship patterns become just another status symbol of your success, so remember to keep in touch with your feelings and emotions so as to avoid becoming cold hearted and methodical. It would really be a symbol of personal security were you to ensure that your success was also the mutual success of your partner. There will be a strong drive for power and public recognition on the grounds that to be successful your professional life should lead to a meaningful contribution to society in a way that brings positive transformation, both personally and at the larger level. This position brings the willpower and drive necessary to reform existing social structures and transform them into something more appropriate for the modern world.

Pluto in the eleventh house

This position will find itself ranging from the radical loner on the one hand convinced that they are on a self-appointed mission to transform humankind, to the obsessive community networker who doesn't know when to stop and who always puts the needs of others before themselves. It is your interactions not just at the personal but also at the external and social level that shape your future. There sometimes can be a deep aversion to groups or organizations of any kind almost to the point of isolation.

Alternatively, any such group you become involved in will be either for intense personal growth or else centred around social change and revising society in some manner and as you age you will find that your personal relationships become more and more friendly, with common social interests. You and your partner may meet, exhibit and deal with many of your power issues within the social sphere that you mutually inhabit, whether that is the Darby and Joan Club or Swingers International, particularly around special interest groups. You are not the type of person to sit on the sidelines if you are part of a group especially if something could be done more effectively and efficiently. Pluto in the eleventh house is not quite leadership material but consistent and regular application makes you a valued and appreciated member of every group you find yourself involved with.

If you have not developed a strong sense of your own ideals and beliefs then you may fall under the influence of others who don't necessarily have your best interests at heart but the opposite side of the same coin is that as long as you feel that you have back up you can be a highly influential instigator of social change. With Pluto in the eleventh house of ideals and community opportunities for transforming or regenerating yourself and your most intimate relationships may come through powerful friends or group associates. There will be a popular side to your nature that makes your company quite sought after but remember not to milk this too much because popularity can be like fame, i.e. fleeting.

You are fiercely loyal to the people of the moment and to those you believe in but you can also be ruthless in pursuing your goals and objectives and releasing others who have fulfilled their purpose. Your expectations can be high, demanding a lot from yourself and others but at the same time you can inspire great admiration from others, or opposition if you adopt a dictatorial attitude. Always listen to your partner's advice and most of the time take it. Let them rule the roost in the bedroom, leaving you free to concentrate on the outside world.

Pluto in the twelfth house

What is this fear business anyway? Other people and both your and their external environments just represent a symbolic shape of what it is that really intimidates you; the suggestion here is not so much fear of other or others, or anything tangible, but fear of being afraid, fear of the unknown and the unknowable. There will certainly be a deep interest in secrets, the underworld, the un and subconscious and anything hidden or concealed. Intuition, empathy and dream analysis are powerful and helpful ways of understanding the language of the depths, certainly there is the potential to be exceptionally perceptive intuitively. Unfortunately, often this can take the form of wild or unfettered imagination and fantasy to the point where the boundaries between reality and fantasy can become very interwoven, leading to personal self-doubt and thus vulnerability to inappropriate influences from others. You really are a walking psychic sponge, soaking up everybody else's grief to the point of almost victimhood or martyrdom. Your emotions and subconscious energies may at times seem complex and this reflects into your one-to-one relationships which go through occasional periods of crisis or trauma as a test of validity and current value, so every so often you will need occasional quiet moments to build your power.

With Pluto in your twelfth house you may be tempted to repress or suppress your emotions in your most personal relationships in case something unexpected comes up. Of course it won't but there is always the background feeling of 'what if', which makes it difficult to really trust someone with your soul until you have known them a long time, at least seven years. In rare examples there can be problems with depression or addictive behaviours, particularly those which have to do with those deep needs that spring from the shadowy side of yourself. Sometimes trusted partners have a clearer perspective on yourself than you do and perhaps they should be listened to more! Old resentments can fester, acting in a way that undermines your ability to trust your inner self, so be aware of this and do your best to live in the present.

In the bedroom, extremes are best avoided despite the temptation, as sometimes Pluto here can hurtle recklessly into the bottomless hole that the twelfth house can represent. Through managing all of your relationships in a transparent and easy way, through remembering to laugh at your own inanities and through keeping life as simple as possible you will find increasingly that opportunities for transforming and regenerating yourself come into the mix and that without even trying you become an inspiration for others. There is a need to feel useful whether to partner and/or society, to stand up for the downtrodden and to feel as though one is contributing on the grounds that this brings more solidity and consistency into your world.

The positive aspects to Pluto

If Pluto is strongly aspected in a favourable way, i.e. by sextile or trine, then as one ages so the awareness of things in your life such as self-confidence, self-awareness and self-belief becomes progressively more noticeable and the ability to stand firm and resolute in the face of challenge or opposition becomes steadily more pronounced. These are the people who would make good police officers, private detectives, pathologists or morticians, forensic accountants, researchers, investigative reporters and psychologists as they get older. Sometimes, Pluto by aspect can bring an immense amount of power into the individual's life as dictated by the houses that the aspect is in but it does take a considerable amount of willpower and self-discipline to turn this into a force for good through the process of regeneration, renewal and eventually transformation. This ultimately leads to rebirth in a number of different ways, whether mental, emotional psychological and/or physical.

The neutral aspects to Pluto

If Pluto is quiet in an individual's chart, i.e. there are no major or strong significant aspects that play a major role in defining personality, then the person will show little if any sign of wishing to go beyond the 'norm' as far as sexual experimentation goes, they will be relatively happy with the status quo and not seek to open up any caverns that they find boarded up in either their or their partner's psyches. There can be little concern or even ignorance about the darker sides of life and an almost innocent side to the personality that has little care or concern for the more psychological influences. To these people, the element of simplicity in their lives is paramount and in many ways their philosophy is 'if it's working, don't fix it'.

The difficult aspects to Pluto

If Pluto makes difficult aspect to either Venus or Mars in your chart or for that matter any of the personal planets then be aware that this is where the 'hard stuff' lies. The squares and oppositions from Pluto to planets in your horoscope show the capacity for phobia and paranoia when young, leading to life or death power struggles as one ages and only by surviving these does one learn the true lesson of a difficult Pluto, to recognise that you are the steward and conduit of power, not the owner. You are more full of power as opposed to powerful and holding that power carries with it an obligation not to let it overpower you and to use it for non-selfish good in the world. Sometimes only by acting as an agent of change and transformation in other people's lives can you really fix your own which is why those people that come through difficult Pluto times invariably turn to helping others in some type of counsellor, therapist or best friend mode.

The conjunction of Pluto to personal planets can also be seen as a challenging aspect if one gives in to the more compulsive or obsessive side of this influence instead of using it as a force for transformation and rebirth. The following list of meanings for the aspects between Venus, Mars and Pluto is by no means complete and should only be used as a guide.

Pluto in aspect to Venus or Mars

Pluto's interaction with sex as represented astrologically by the influences of Venus and Mars is not for the fainthearted as it can bring up all types of ghosties and fears from the long past, although generally these fears and complexes don't usually arise until the individual is ready to deal with them. Periodically sudden crisis and trauma can bring dramatic psychological change into some people's lives. There are perhaps three generalised basic types of Plutonian personality when it comes to sex and these types are determined not only by the house position of Pluto but also by the aspects of Pluto to other points in your horoscope, particularly Venus and Mars. The aspects between Pluto and other planets, particularly the Sun and the Moon, dictate issues of identity, individuality and purpose and fall outside of the remit of this book but the aspects of Pluto to Venus and Mars show the ways in which we as individuals respond to the more psychological, deep and basic sides of our procreative and physical nature.

Pluto in aspect to Venus

These two planetary energies do not normally sit very well together as the gentler and receptive side of Venus can have difficulty in dealing and coping with the almost unstoppable drive and energy of Pluto, emanating from within your own un and subconscious. Difficult manifestations of this energy can be seen in some people's almost obsessive desire for money or possessions or else the inability to rely on your relationships, inevitably leading to paranoia and phobia around trust issues. There can be extreme belief in your convictions and opinions to the point of ostracization and an incredible amount of stubbornness. In the worst cases this position has no scruples about acting in an underhand way if the end justifies the means and integrity and dignity can be a foreign land.

There is another side to this combination, which when working well brings an unswerving degree of loyalty and a willingness to stand by their partner no matter what as long as they themselves are being dealt with honestly. It brings resolve, determination, depth and a willingness to look at all the difficult issues as opposed to sweeping them under the table. There can be a latent passion here that rides almost unknowingly on the waves emanating from deep within themselves and once they learn to trust their physical bodies these people can become consummate and willing lovers. Just don't ever lie to them.

Pluto in aspect to Mars

Potentially these are the two most warlike planetary energies and certainly the two that deal most of all with anger but they also deal with ways of expressing yourself that conveys not just power over but power within. The sensible people with Mars/Pluto aspects know that they are not the owner of the power that flows through them, merely the steward and the conduit. Not so much powerful, as full of power. These aspects can bring the nihilistic, the destructive and the violent to the surface but equally as strongly it can represent self-mastery, such as martial arts, archery or some other form of directed physical expression that uses both power and skill as an aid to focus and concentration. If people with Mars/Pluto connections don't acknowledge within themselves the element of power that flows through them and instead either ignore or suppress it, then that same power will come out in ways such as anger, accident, poison, zits, acne or some other form of physical injury or disability.

Rarely do Mars/Pluto people have steady and stable lifestyles. Instead, they find that periodically they have to make certain choices or take specific actions and at the end of the day it's better to act than it is to react. There is a need for relative caution with the bedroom as the raw power of these people can at times be quite overwhelming. They can keep going for hours, lack of stamina is not a problem here. In fact, it can be the opposite in that they can burn their partners out if they are not careful. Wise and judicious usage of physical energy is advised here, it's better to be a laser or a scalpel as opposed to a sledgehammer or a battering ram.

Pluto sextile Venus or Mars

The sextile aspect is that of sixty degrees, one sixth of a circle between the two planets in question. This links planets in signs that are compatible with each other, creating a healthy working dynamic. The key word here is 'opportunity' and the sextile is seen as a very favourable aspect. Seeing as one of the planets involved here is Pluto, the opportunity in question will be one eventually leading to some form of harmonic transformation. There will be the occasional opportunity in life to transform, regenerate and purify the state of love and relationships in your life without going through much of the trauma that others seem to go through.

Venus sextile Pluto gives strong feelings and perceptions, it deepens your response to love, people and life in general and brings out any intrinsic artistic talents you may possess by producing original creativity. The key to success in relationships with this aspect is through your understanding of people and their motivations; it brings out the potential to see the best in everyone and gives you an aura of seemingly powerful and magnetic popularity, almost as if you have a completely non-judgmental magical charm for dealing with people. You may find that you are easily attracted by appearance and sex appeal yet just as quickly turned off by superficiality.

Venus working so well with Pluto brings the capacity to love deeply, passionately and wholeheartedly and others may find your intensity either extremely attractive or else rather threatening. When you get involved with someone you can really pour yourself into them with limitless energy, although this energy evaporates into other creative or artistic areas of life when you aren't involved with anyone. There is a deeply sensual charisma and you can have a powerful emotional influence on others, especially on the opposite sex, and it may be that you use your attractiveness to subtly manipulate others without even realising it. The understanding and appreciation of love is instinctive and you are fully prepared to accept the responsibilities of love as well as the joys, as long as there is a healthy result at the end of the day.

Pluto sextile Mars brings a high level of physical vitality. There should be a healthy and positive approach to all forms of sexual expression and you perceive sex in natural and organic terms without inner compulsions or old patterns distorting energy release. This aspect produces dominantly strong willpower and forcefulness in style that gets to the bottom of the most complex issue, giving you the ability to read people and their motives well. There is an expectancy of honesty in your dealings with people, preferring to hear the truth rather than be confused by evasion or psychological manipulation. Honesty is one of your most highly valued qualities and you can be very persuasive in the way that you express your opinions. You will also have a grasp of dramatic presentation with which you can influence others and don't have any problems with taking calculated chances. It normally brings with it great sexual stamina and a perseverant quality that doesn't really stop until objectives have been realised. There will be decisiveness but no confrontation or conflict in your ways of resolving problems. Usually others know where you stand, you are not shy of revealing your viewpoints and you expect the same of others, whether that is in the outside world or in the privacy of the bedroom.

Pluto trine Venus or Mars

The difference between a sextile from Pluto and a trine from Pluto is minor but succinct. A sextile is an aspect of the potential for opportunity but an opportunity that has to be taken and worked at in order to be successful, whereas a trine is far more giving and generous; it gives a natural and organic talent that can sometimes be so latent as to be unrecognised. Perhaps the only drawback with trines is that they can make you complacent if you take things for granted.

The trine formed between Venus and Pluto in an individual chart shows an intense romantic nature with a fundamental faith in life, an innate optimism that all will work out well in the end. Giving similar indications to the sextile where the possibility of personal transformation is likely to occur through emotional experiences of a higher and intense kind, especially through the shape and form of personal one-to-one relationship, there is likely to be the feeling that higher values are essential in interpersonal relationships and you try to embody these in your own life. You may have to avoid a tendency to interfere in others' choices and let them find their own way even when it hurts to do so. This is one of those aspects where you meet people and you instantly feel as if you have known them all of your life, if not longer, bringing instant recognition. It's not as though you are waiting for Mr or Ms Right but this aspect does give you the ability to recognise a fated quality of interaction and attraction when you see it. This belief in the goodness of life can be 'contagious', and you may be attracted towards sharing your personal approach or philosophy of life with your significant other. You are more than capable of seeing that the bedrock of a partnership, apart from mutual love and affection, lies in qualities of commitment, transparency, honesty, integrity, responsibility to mutual obligations and allowing each other the space to express his or her own unique nature with a degree of both autonomy and privacy.

Pluto trine Mars is a more proactive business making you a passionate person capable of generating a commanding aura and a strong degree of confidence about your own talents and an intense personal power and immense energy as well as an assertive nature. You should recognise within yourself a knack for uncovering things and bring up things from the underworld or from the distant past and are excellent at exposing secrets, making you a natural investigator or researcher, relentless in pursuit of your goal and never giving up. When difficulties arise, you prefer to avoid conflict and confrontation in favour of more peaceful or subtle methods of resolving problems but the furthest that you will go is halfway because any further would be surrender and it's more your style at that point to just walk away with your head held high. There is the capacity for applying tremendous effort to anything you attempt.

A trine between Mars and Pluto enables you to draw on deep reserves of energy to get through any crisis and your physical and sexual drives and desires are likely to be not only strong and intense much of the time but also controlled and purposeful. Romantic connections have deep meaning and interest and will not be entered into lightly. You don't do light-hearted flirtatiousness, finding it superficial and vacuous. There will be the ability to act quickly in any emergency and to make far-reaching decisions and commitments that others may require a long time to consider, that's why this aspect is relatively common in the charts of firefighters, police officers and paramedics.

Pluto square Venus or Mars

A square is a very different affair to a sextile or a trine. Whereas the sextile and trine are flowing and generally beneficial aspects, the square definitely is not. It is a hard angle of ninety degrees that creates stress and tension and often manifests as direct problems or challenges. However, you are never given the problems in your chart without also being given the opportunity to turn them into gifts but squares in particular can be very hard work. A square from Pluto to either Venus or Mars will bring a degree of intensity and extremism into all of your one-to-one relationship patterns across the board in a way that almost always manifests as serious challenge, especially when younger.

The fundamental difference between Pluto square Venus and Pluto square Mars is that the latter is more given to direct action, confrontation or even aggression/violence whilst the former is likely to be more insidious, emotionally manipulative and coercive, although these are broad assumptions and should only be taken as such.

Pluto square Venus

In an attempt to control the outcome of a relationship or the loved one's feelings, there can sometimes be the tendency to turn to manipulative games.

You are certainly capable of being a powerful manipulator and can often try to make things appear a certain way. Even if you do succeed at this there is never the feeling that you have won and this type of behaviour feeds a vicious cycle that you should avoid getting yourself into from the very start of a relationship, because otherwise you might attract intense encounters that have love-hate themes as a result.

You will meet your darker side or inner demons through your relationships and it is critical that you recognise this as your 'stuff' and not project it onto your partner. Letting go of a relationship can be hard for you to do and you can easily pressure the partner into doing things that save you from acting so be careful not to let your relationships get to a point where your partner is superfluous or superficial. What you want is often not what you need so as you strive to satisfy your desires you may also have to endure periodic degrees of suffering. At times you could be obsessed with using sex as a device to obtain financial security or material comforts, although again this doesn't have a realistic long-term future as far as personal contentment or happiness is concerned.

There is a thin line between love and hate and your potential for extremes of behaviour and sexual intensity can lead you into the wrong kinds of relationships, especially when younger. Certainly you will learn much about yourself through your relationships and you may not always like what you see, finding that again when young there can be a tendency to get tied down to a pattern of endless repetition in relationships and experience difficulty in letting go even when situations are at their most painful.

Venus squaring Pluto can be almost masochistic in nature where it occasionally feels that it is only through the pain of rejection or some form of torment that you can feel alive. Obviously this type of energy won't last long before burn out or madness occur so don't let yourself get dragged obsessively down over a period of time. Love and power can easily become confused with one another and one of the things you may become aware of as you age is that your relationships reflect your own inner turmoil.

The other side of the same coin is that as soon as you start respecting yourself as you are now, you will find that you attract a giving, loving person more easily and better-quality relationships will ensue as a result. The relationship that you have with 'other' will be a direct mirror image of the relationship that you have with yourself. Marriage could occur out of a need for financial or emotional security, although personal security without unconditional love is more of a prison than a godsend.

Patronizing people is a poor substitute for being honest with them, so don't make promises unless you intend to keep them. A square between Venus and Pluto suggests that your emotional life may at times be subject to many problems, many of these relating to various sexual issues. This aspect can be symbolic of intense emotional and sexual involvements and sometimes this can be with very debasing influences. At the end of the day if you have got Venus and Pluto square in your chart be clear not only with others but also with yourself about the difference between your needs, wants and desires and how far you will go to achieve them. Treat others the way you would like to be treated by them and keep things as clean as you can. You can easily go down into your own Hadean cans of worms with this aspect or you can aspire to fly phoenix-like into the highest and cleanest forms of pure love imaginable. Just don't sell your soul for comfort.

Pluto square Mars

This is one of the hardest aspects in the entire zodiac to deal with. It brings up issues of anger, rage and even violence in ways that can lead you to being out of control if you are not careful. The square between Mars and Pluto produces a forceful nature and power struggles seem to be a common theme in your life, regardless of whom the actual struggle is with. There may be anger control issues; there can be a number of major clashes and sudden changes, often with very damaging results and possibly even violent or aggressive outbursts. You can be very intense and passionate but also can sabotage yourself in a moment of passion. This aspect suggests a strong sex drive that may not be well controlled at times, giving a need to rein in your overly assertive nature occasionally, otherwise power struggles and control issues may surface in your relationships.

The interactions that you share with your significant other reflect the relationship that you have with yourself. The better you treat yourself, the more successful your relationships. Your approach to love and sex can be quite intense at times as your sexual nature can be very strong, which adds a very magnetic quality to your appeal. When someone finds you attractive it can transform into near obsession, either towards or from you, or sometimes both (fun for a brief time but obsession normally doesn't last long). Whether you realise it or not you tend to come across as stronger than you intend and there can be a tendency to impose your will upon others which can cause severe problems for yourself when they react in self-defence, resulting in both of your personal boundaries being tested.

There can be a distinctly possessive and demanding streak in your sexual nature so be aware of your effect on others. Despite the attraction to people whom may not have as much vitality as yourself, your best compatibility is with someone who is as feisty and competitive as you. Yes, you will fight a lot like cat and dog but you will both find in each other someone psychologically powerful and hopefully equal. When it happens, the sex will be primal, raw, passionate, powerful and hot. Some people can be really intimidated by you and you may not understand why.

Look at your issues of fear and abandonment. You want a deep, soulful attachment on a sexual level and as you don't take rejection well there can be a fear of betrayal and abandonment and this can change the way that you see people, making it too easy for you to find something negative about them. Find a way to convince others to work with you of their own free will on the grounds that it's better to have them pissing on the inside of the tent as opposed to the outside. This is the same principle as keeping your friends close but your enemies closer. You have a strong urge to act out your fantasies or to live your dream and you will do things that others only talk or dream about but bear in mind the effect of your actions on others and behave in ways that you would like others to behave towards you. Take this into the bedroom and you can find yourself being the dynamic, coarse and initiatory, or else someone incredibly sophisticated, finely tuned and specialist. The choice is yours but the latter approach does have more long-term benefits.

Would you rather be a lump hammer or a laser? Ask your partner for the answer to that question…

You perceive the cruel edge in people and understand its source because you can recognise the same energy within yourself so as you deal with your own ruthlessness you can learn how to respond to it in others without risking either yours or others' physical well-being but there is no way that you will easily tolerate a dominating attitude in others. There is respect for power and authority but only if it is handled fairly. This is the hardest of positions for Mars and Pluto, you have to deal with power head on and either rise to become empowered or else let yourself become consumed and absorbed by other people's power over you in some way. The simple and basic principle in all of your dealings with others and their dealings with you should be that 'if you always tell the truth, you never have to remember what you have said'.

Pluto opposite Venus or Mars

When two planets are on opposite sides of the heavens to each other with the Earth in the middle of the straight line between them they are said to be in opposition to each other. 'Opposites attract' is an old metaphor and in some cases it is clearly true. In the case of Pluto opposing either Venus or Mars the opposition is clearly defined as troublesome and challenging, due at least partly to the huge amount of unconscious and subconscious patterns brought to the surface with this aspect.

On the one hand there will be Venus or Mars, looking to be balanced in gender polarity and healthy in terms of both sexual and sensual expression, and on the other hand there is Pluto, normally the planet signifying obsession and compulsion, intensity and extremes and the occasional period of crisis and/or trauma. He is also associated with the regenerative and transformational sides of life, refining, purging and purifying through the process of elimination. Pluto erupts from the underworld occasionally and if there are any suppressed or repressed issues that have not been dealt with, they will also suddenly come out onto the world stage at the same time. People with the opposition of Pluto to either Venus or Mars will often experience these suppressed or repressed issues as manifesting through their relationships with significant other, sometimes to the point of compulsion/obsession or even different levels of confrontation or aggression, although this is normally more verbal and emotional as opposed to physical.

In the bedroom this can manifest as periodical power struggles based around surrender and control. The more any of these tendencies are suppressed or ignored the more danger there is of these sides of yourself emerging in less manageable or pleasant ways. Yet obviously these same tendencies cannot be pandered to without them emerging as major external life influences, something not desirable in a sane society. The easiest way to manage these challenging influences is to build into your relationship with your partner the trust and understanding that allows mutual expression of game or role playing within the bedroom in a safe and boundaried way. This brings the willingness and urge to express yourself in necessary ways that otherwise may be repressed, leading to potential psychological challenges further on down the line.

The nature of power cannot be ignored and, in some cases, must be met head on, although this is usually more common with Mars than with Venus. Outside of the bedroom, the opposition to Venus or Mars from Pluto often manifests as deep-rooted unconscious rebellion or resentment towards all systems of authoritarian (normally male) role model. You may be perfectly conventional on the outside but as soon as someone who has not earned your respect starts telling you what to do the subversive side of your nature comes out to play big time, regardless of whether it is employer, parent, teacher or partner. Far better perhaps to corral this energy and put it into something positive and creative such as some form of disciplined martial art or other physical and focussed ability. It is in the opposition aspect along with the conjunction that the starker differences between Venus and Mars become obvious, with the more receptive/passive and projective/assertive sides of these aspects amplified.

Pluto opposite Venus

In the bedroom they can play the role of the tramp, the gigolo or the surrender junkie with ease, at times it is almost as though they will be anything you want them to be in order to be accepted. It makes for a highly emotional disposition that on the negative side tries to remould the partner into something more to your own liking as opposed to compromising and meeting partners half way. The opposite and positive side of this is the ability to help both partner and self go through the fear and pain barriers together knowing that the true and deep love offered by this position will always bring a symbiosis at the intimate level that takes the interaction way beyond that of normal relationship.

This position often has clear definitions with sex. It's either a relatively quick, functional need being met and/or brief desire being sated or else it's the deep, committed and passionate loving experience of which sex is only the physical but this experience can take years of both practice and trust to evolve into.

Venus opposite Pluto has a kind of Scorpionic feel to it that on the surface challenges you to understand what is going on underneath, a kind of 'I dare you to work me out' game. It likes to drag partners under the quilt and pretend that they are in a cave or even better, to be not pretending and in the real thing. This aspect has a considerable degree of the extremist about it but not so much in a threatening or challenging way as much as a seductive and suggestive way that is never totally clear or transparent.

The nature of Venus and Pluto in opposition is to look for the crevices where dirt can be hiding, to go the extra mile to uncover and find out about partner and to insinuate itself into everything around itself, to have a little awareness of everything and everyone in the immediate environment. It helps make these potentially paranoid people feel safe as though they have a grip on the situation. Woe betide anyone who pokes too deep into their personal lives without permission and when dealing with these highly charged and sensual people never kiss and tell or be prepared to be frozen out for life if you do. What can come across as secrecy is actually the privacy born of past experiences of deceit and mistrust.

This position truly can be the ice maiden, the unbreakable and the involatile, with an impenetrable wall being the only possible interface between them and the people they distrust. It can also be the most passionate and loving when it feels both safe to do so and wanted at the same time.

On the surface level everything can seem to be constantly a game with different levels of intrigue and trust and over the years associated with long-term relationships these people learn and accept the need to let others have the upper hand occasionally, just so that at least Venus opposite Pluto can satisfy itself that it's not being a total control freak. They don't do lightweight people or partners; they tend to go for the deep thinkers of the zodiac, people with substance and solidity. At the root of their fear lies the issue of abandonment so the sensible ones with this position partner themselves with someone who can be strong for them when they can't do it for themselves, someone who will take their anger and then still be there to hug and cuddle them regardless. Secretly they ooze passion and sensuality but they need to feel safe enough both with self and with partner in order to express it and that safety takes not only a secure environment but also the stability of years of experience.

Pluto opposite Mars

This aspect is perhaps one of most challenging of all in terms of anger management, physical expression and the transformational processes of life. The majority of people with this position are likely to have experienced a significant level of difficulty with one or both of the parents in the early years and unless acknowledged and dealt with early in life this energy then builds into a resentment against all forms of imposed or disciplined structures. This is not the position of the rebel fighting for a better future but more the position of the destroyer, willing to bring down the old to see if something new and better comes out of the mix.

Mars opposite Pluto doesn't really do words, except in short sentences. It generally works on the principle that whilst constant and regular action is the desired outcome, when necessary specific actions always speak louder than words. This capacity for incisiveness and direct action is normally only activated by external pressure and it is a measure of the person's maturity and evolution as to whether they express this action in ways that are either destructive or transformative. Parents of children with this aspect are advised to get them into some type of assertive and projective martial art on the grounds that it will train them not only physically but also mentally. Children of parents with this aspect are advised to suggest to them that some type of passive and receptive form of martial art, such as Tai Chi or Qi Gong would bring an element of balance into their lives.

In the outside world Mars opposite Pluto manifests in a number of different ways but the common factor here is that of an unstoppable drive towards whatever the person considers to be success in their life. If untrained or repressed this energy of anger can emerge into the world in a number of challenging ways from generally surly and resentful behaviour to almost aggressive attitudes. Commonly these people work alone if only for the reason that most other people can't keep up with their output. These are the people who if they can focus and train their energy away from anger into specialization are capable of becoming true masters of their ability.

When there is no vehicle for focus the Mars/Pluto energy can turn inwards and fester, occasionally erupting in acts or words of seemingly irrational and unconscious anger. These are the people who go in for marathons or similar other forms of pushing their boundaries via willpower and pure determination. If they can divert their energy into their work by doing something as a career that is representative of the Mars/Pluto urge for in depth action they can transform both their own and potentially many other people's lives as well. The challenge here is not so much that of finding your specialist niche because that will occur one way or another in the course of time: it is knowing when to let yourself stop being that specialist and sit back and smell the roses and the coffee. Perhaps the biggest danger to yourself here is that of burn out, of not knowing when to stop.

In the privacy of the bedroom, Mars opposite Pluto will have any different number of expressive forms but none of them will be passive for that long without wanting to take action. These people are not going to be content with sex as a mechanism for sharing love. To them sex is a quick way into the state of consciousness where they can feel and surf the flow of the true power of life, although what they do when in that state of feeling is dependent on their personal moralistic code.

Here lies the aggressive and violent, the manipulative and the coercive as well as the selfish and amoral attitude of the emotionally corrupt or unevolved, based purely and solely on power over others as a survival mechanism. Here also lies the aspirant grail knight who purges and purifies themselves of all that is corrupt and dirty, who constantly seeks to transform their raw lust and desire and regenerate it into something far more refined and sophisticated. There is a need for physical expression at a constant level with this position whilst at the same time struggling to live within your own boundaries as opposed to those imposed on you by others and this physical expression, whether sex, athletics, martial arts or other will inevitably become the vehicle of personal transformation.

Pluto conjunct Venus or Mars

The idea of either of Venus or Mars being conjunct with Pluto in a person's chart adds a deeper and darker dimension to the analysis, it compels the individual to face and deal with experiences of direct power. This power can be self-empowerment where your ability to make and take actions and decisions makes you a no-nonsense kind of person and people will quickly know where they stand with you. Or this can be other people attempting to hold some type of manipulative or otherwise inappropriate power in your life which unfortunately is far too common. The power of the conjunction makes the realisation of the flow of power through your life inevitable, it's what you do with it that counts, not how much you have. A conjunction can be an incisive and accurate point of specific timing and event or it can represent a blunt and misdirected yet powerful force that can blunder about the place aimlessly.

As far as the bedroom goes, this aspect brings a focussed and concentrated stamina into the sexual and sensual arena, giving you a powerfully charged aura and a magnetic and charismatic personality. Sex will never be just light-hearted fun, it will always have an element of depth, mystery and communion with the unknowable about it, almost shamanistic. Pluto conjuncting Venus often describes what you really want and desire and Pluto conjuncting Mars shows the ways and the levels at which you will operate to make those desires come true. The most powerful of people with Venus or Mars on top of Pluto are those strong enough to surrender to the unknown and the unknowable, especially to their partners, knowing that they are invulnerable yet able to grow with partner in a way they couldn't do alone. Willing to explore every possible taboo and boundary they insist only on privacy and trust as absolutes. These are the archetypal 'forgive but never forget' types of individuals. Just don't treat them as lightweights because they don't hang around for long if you do.

In day-to-day operations these aspects have a lot to do with inter personal dynamics, with people in the workplace, on the street, in your social sense and in the family as much as in your personal and intimate relationships. People will experience you as a hard hitter in life, not someone to be trifled with or dealt with as being insubstantial. There will be an intensity to your gaze which can unnerve the fainthearted and sometimes your silence speaks volumes. You convey a sense of 'knowing' without any rational reason for that assumption. This certainly has the effect of sorting the wheat from the chaff and keeping the wimps as well as the vampires at the door but it can also make you feel isolated to a degree. This is an excellent position for undercover work, research, working in the depths, or psychology but the way that you manifest these urges will depend on which of Venus or Mars is involved and what signs and houses of the zodiac are involved. What to others may seem an almost compulsive degree of fascination with a particular subject or person is to you an area of concentration, focus and hopefully, successful specialisation.

Pluto conjunct Venus

The core root meaning of this conjunction is that of desperation to be loved, to be wanted and to be judged and found to be of value and worth. Most people with this position do anything and everything to find a position in the world where they are held as being of substance, of worth at the material and physical level, whereas the sensible ones know that the true arbiter and judge of value and worth is through the eyes of yourself, not others. Even the more highly evolved people with this position will still have a judgement system but at the end of the day what is it that is really of value and worth?

Venus conjunct Pluto will bring you ever more deeper and revelatory experiences and understandings which serve to broaden both your taste and knowledge. What you do with this is obviously up to you but the cleaner you keep things the easier new things, events and developments become and the more complicated or underhand things get the more the quicksand and treacle thickens. Power brings with it responsibility to behave in an ethical manner.

As far as eroticism goes Venus conjunct Pluto likes to think that it wrote the training manual and all the updates and no one should try and convince them otherwise without sting proof armour. These are the people who use sex as a vehicle to a higher level of sensuality where they just drift and dream along in bliss but then they have to come back down to grim reality when the partner moves or the bladder calls and the return to physical reality can sometimes be a let-down. In truth this position is more given to the sensual than the sexual; one is the result of the other. These people value their partners for their subtlety, their sensuality and their refined passion as much as their raw sex appeal. It is the hint of mystery, the allure and the potential seductive sides of life that epitomise the elegance of Venus with the mystique and danger of Pluto and the blending of the two brings a subtle, mysterious and ever so slightly dangerous element into the equation.

As they age, people with Venus conjunct Pluto become more concerned about the quality of experience as much as, if not more so than, the quantity. They go for the peak of experiences, those that they will remember for the rest of their life and their attitude can be all or nothing at times, preferring to go for the one memorable time as opposed to lots of mundane occasions. There will always be the desire to peel away and penetrate the different layers of the onion that lie in relationship patterns, both personal and otherwise, but this is done in such a subversive and unconscious way that the recipient doesn't even realise that they are being probed until it's over, if then. There is a charming and seductive manner that beguiles people into sharing their deepest secrets but in the same moment these at times implacable people are not that good at talking about their own feelings and emotions until they feel safe enough with you to do so. The way to their heart is through your conscious and willing acceptance of them as they are and your constant assurance that they are more than good enough in your eyes. Then you will have the most devoted and passionate partner you could ever ask for and you will both be really happy. This really is the 'warts and all' position.

Pluto conjunct Mars

When Mars ruling your physical, projective, sexual and assertive nature is in the same place as Pluto ruling your more unconscious urges and your psychological well-being, a powerful blend of energy occurs which can't be denied, blocked or shelved and must be dealt with. It creates a dogmatic and somewhat bloody-minded attitude to getting things done and depending on the sign and house of the zodiac that the conjunction is in will give a powerhouse of unstoppable energy into your life. It does not bring subtlety or tact with it, indeed these may come towards the bottom of the list of attributes. Mars/Pluto is very no nonsense and prefers to deal with yes or no, black or white. It is not really bothered as long as there is clarity. This combination has a quality of ruthlessness about it but normally this is shown towards yourself more than it is to others.

In the primacy of the bedroom there is likely to be a degree of extremism from the primal and basic urges of life to the epitome of sophistication, stopping at all points in between. Mars conjunct Pluto evokes passion and sexuality in its rawest and most basic form, where the instinctual and the primal are as important as the intuitive and sophisticated and never does things by half measures. It brings lust into the equation either as a tool for self-expression and mutual pleasure or as a tool for control or domination. People with this aspect are advised to keep a quality of transparency about them with their partners as this precludes any potential misunderstanding.

When older and having survived the rigours of youth, people with Mars and Pluto in the same place generally become more and more specialised as they age. Here you find the best surgeons, the greatest scientists and the most visionary architects, those who go the extra mile to get their point across and come across to the world as sharp, effective and efficient. These are the people who cut through the crap and deliberately orchestrate their lives in a way that says that they don't have any time to waste on superficialities. Their ability to make decisions in an almost forensic way normally precludes mistakes; they seem to have an added edge when looking at problems or doubts. At the same time, there is a need to know when to stop because if they don't take time out to enjoy the company of others, they may rapidly find themselves alone or even lonely, simply because they burn the rest of the world out.

For The Curious

I've been aware of Astrology since 1977 and properly conscious of its influence since 1980. I started doing paid astrological readings in 1983 and since the year 2000 giving readings to clients has been my only source of income. It is from this large database of population of different gender, age group, ethnicity, nationality and philosophy that I have formed my ideas in this book, although I must acknowledge anonymously those clients and friends who have helped with specific sections pertaining to them.

As an active environmentalist as well as an astrologer, I have a commitment to improving the quality of life for all life forms on this planet and as far as humanity goes it seems to me that the emerging ideas concerning the imminent 'consciousness re-evolution' are probably the best bet as far as a realistic future goes. In that context, astrology and humour combined are an excellent teaching tool of consciousness. The horoscope teaches you to know yourself, nothing more and nothing less. I truly believe that if astrology were taught in schools, within two generations we would see an end to war, politics and religious indoctrination.

Acknowledgements

My thanks go to many people too numerous to name but there are three in particular. James, who helped me get the courage of my convictions and opened my eyes to some of the bigger pictures in the world. There is Ginny from New England who really gets my humour and helped out with the fine tuning. And Karen. Without her assistance and encouragement, none of this would have been possible.

Printed in the USA
CPSIA information can be obtained
at www.ICGtesting.com
LVHW052049051223
765654LV00002B/292